REGRET-FREE
LIVING

REGRET

STEPHEN ARTERBURN

WITH JOHN SHORE

FREE LIVING

HOPE FOR PAST MISTAKES AND FREEDOM FROM UNHEALTHY PATTERNS

BETHANY HOUSE PUBLISHERS

Minneapolis, Minnesota

Published by Bethany House Publishers
11400 Hampshire Avenue South
Bloomington, Minnesota 55438

Bethany House Publishers is a division of
Baker Publishing Group, Grand Rapids, Michigan.

Printed in the United States of America

Library of Congress Cataloging-in-Publication Data

Arterburn, Stephen.
    Regret-free living : hope for past mistakes and freedom from unhealthy patterns / Stephen Arterburn with John Shore.
      p.   cm.
    ISBN 978-0-7642-0424-1 (hardcover : alk. paper)   1. Interpersonal relations—Religious aspects—Christianity. 2. Regret—Religious aspects—Christianity. I. Shore, John, 1958– II. Title.
    BV4597.52.A78   2009
    248.4—dc22

2009025241

■   ■   ■

To

MIKE

the man with no regrets

■   ■   ■

Books by

Stephen Arterburn

with John Shore

FROM BETHANY HOUSE PUBLISHERS

....

*Being Christian**

Being Christian Workbook

*Midlife Manual for Men**

Midlife Manual for Men Workbook

Regret-Free Living

* Audio CD, DVD, & Group Leader's Kit also available

CONTENTS

Introduction

As radio host of *New Life Live,* a daily one-hour call-in show, I can honestly say that at no other time in my life have I heard the voices of more people saturated with regret. When 9/11 occurred, President Bush announced that our world would never be the same. Well, we now must pack carry-on liquids in three-ounce containers, and to be sure, those who were injured or lost loved ones were left with deep wounds. But the rest of us? We really haven't seen much change; there really hasn't been a lot of difference.

We did, however, see the world change—and change very quickly—when the economic downturn (financial disaster) began in 2008. Many who thought they were wise or brilliant investors discovered that someone had made off with every last dollar. Some millionaires and billionaires were wiped out within a few months. Some who were ready to retire changed plans and set about to work the rest of their lives. People who'd had six-figure salaries were interviewed in lines at shelters. Homes were lost, dreams were shattered, and the number of corporate greed's innocent victims swelled beyond belief.

The losses and collapses have been dramatic and agonizing; many people are steeped in regret that they hadn't seen it coming. They're often stunned that they'd been so presumptuous as to assume our economic growth would continue unabated. In portfolios, regrets replaced assets. "If only" has become a mantra for those reliving so many less-than-informed decisions.

For others, the regret path they're walking is not financial but relational. Betrayal, divorce, and all sorts of untreated addictions leave both victim and perpetrator full of regret over the choices they've made.

The Bible tells the story of Esau selling his birthright to Jacob for a mere bowl of soup. According to Hebrews 12, no matter how bad Esau later felt about that deal, no matter how many bitter tears of regret he shed, there was nothing he could do to change what he'd done. Imagine the pain he must have felt, looking back on his terrible swap.

If Esau hadn't been out of control, he would have never offered such a phenomenal bargain. He was controlled by his appetite and desire for immediate relief. And while he looks foolish today, he's no different from the many millions who have walked in his "I want/need it now" shoes.

Most who have struggled with eating disorders can relate to Esau. Those addicted to drugs, who become willing to do anything for relief from withdrawal, understand him. Anyone who's destroyed a marriage over desire for hours with Internet porn knows how Esau could get himself in such a mess.

I certainly know how Esau felt. I know what it's like to obtain instant relief and then discover only a life filled with shameful regret and sorrow, to wake up realizing "*what* a mistake I've made"—and knowing that no matter how much regret I feel, there's nothing I can do to make it right.

■ ■ ■

However, I discovered a way out of shame and regret. I'm not living burdened every day with something God does not want me to carry. I don't wake up every morning thinking God is whispering in my ear, *Okay, Steve, get out there and serve me—and don't forget those horrid, embarrassing choices you made or any of the other stupid things you've done since.*

I'm thankful and amazed that God no longer remembers my sins (see Hebrews 10:17; Jeremiah 31:34).

But before we go further, let me tell you how the most regrettable decision of my life unfolded.

The sad truth (and I've mentioned this before in other books) is that I talked a girlfriend whom I got pregnant into ending the life of our unborn child. I did that because I was selfish. I didn't want anything as life-altering as parenthood to interfere with all my big plans.

Though I hesitate to speak for her, I suppose at heart my girlfriend agreed to the abortion for the same kinds of reasons so many women take that final, irreversible step: She was confused, scared, and unwilling or unprepared to take on the responsibility of a new life. And perhaps worst of all, she was listening and responding to pressure from me.

What I was thinking about most was myself. I'd convinced myself that if I was free to be my own man, I could really make something of my life. I wasn't paying attention to what God wanted for my girlfriend, for me, or for the baby inside of her. I was singing the ugliest song a person can sing: *"Me! Me! Me!"*

It wasn't long after our pregnancy was terminated that I sat alone in my bedroom, hung my head, and cried. I'd finally realized the severity and finality of what I had done. I knew I had taken the life of my child—our child, God's child—and that this was terribly wrong. It was a pain as deep as any I've ever felt. That pain and my secretive response to it led to major health problems (including ulcers) with life-threatening severity.

After several months of suffering, I opened up to my parents and a few others about the abortion. They all treated me lovingly and consolingly, but their shock and anger leaked through their nice words.

Regret from irreversible choices and consequences would become a familiar companion of mine for years to come. Eventually I would try to make it right with the mother of my unborn child, asking for her forgiveness for my selfishness and forcefulness.

She said she forgave me.

But her forgiveness was not enough.

I needed God's forgiveness.

I needed to feel his forgiveness.

And I needed to find some way to forgive myself.

But I couldn't forgive myself. So I continued my detached journey of waking up and then starting, enduring, and ending my day full of inconsolable regret. My shameful ruminations often cut off any meaningful connection with others. I was convinced that I would regret what I had done to my baby every single day for the rest of my life.

As the months and even years passed, I continued to ask myself what, if anything, I could do to relieve myself of regret for the wrong I had done. This nagging question haunted everything I did. I knew God always forgives because of the work of his Son, Jesus Christ, on the cross—but that his forgiveness could be for me, and could extend to this act, was beyond my comprehension. I felt I had gone too far, had committed something beyond God's grace. And to forgive myself without knowing and feeling that God forgave me would be impossible.

What did I have to look forward to besides more mistakes, more sins, more self-condemnation increasing the gap between me and others? Saddled with this heavy burden, I made my way the best I could.

■ ■ ■

Not being able to forgive yourself for your boneheaded, arrogant, and selfish actions is one of the biggest inhibitors to living the life God most wants you to live. If you're always dragging yourself down with the past, how is God going to lift you up in the future? It's easy to kneel in church and hang your head, praying for God to forgive you, but you also must face what you've done and deal with it in a direct and forthright manner. You have to cleanse and prepare yourself so that you'll always be as ready as possible to be the man or woman God intends you to be.

That, my friend, is what this book is here to help you do.

And we should be clear about one thing, right off the bat: There is no way to be alive and avoid doing and saying foolish and even idiotic things, things you're bound to later wish you hadn't done and said at all.

But today is the day for you to begin to unload all the bad feelings and thoughts that come from keeping regret and shame bottled up inside. People, especially men, typically think they can take the bad things they've done and just ignore them all, hoping they'll go away.

The more they try this, the more their regrets and fears compound.

If "stuffing" is what you've done with your guilt, *Regret-Free Living* will show you how to get out your shovel, drop to your knees, and start digging until you've found that awful buried "treasure" inside you. We're going to haul that moldy, smelly old trunk out of the ground, sweep off the dirt and mud, pry it open, and dispose of all the toxic, deteriorated, useless stuff inside.

Maybe the thing you regret involves mistreating a loved one.

Maybe, because it benefited you in some way, you accused someone of doing something you knew they didn't do.

Maybe you took credit for someone else's work.

Maybe you let a little office flirtation turn into something that caused much hurt.

Maybe you made foolish decisions that put you and your family in deep financial trouble.

The list goes on and on and on, doesn't it? And so do the regrets, guilt, and shame that doing those things produces. But it doesn't have to be this way. There's a road out of that terrible, ever-downward spiral.

After I convinced my pregnant girlfriend to end the life of our child, I thought there was no way I'd ever alleviate the inner pain I felt from having encouraged and allowed such a terrible thing. For a long time, everything I did or felt happened in a dark and gloomy shadow.

But you know what? With God's grace, I eventually found the path that led to living without regrets controlling so much of what I did. I discovered that I could come out of any self-created darkness and step back into the light God intended to shine down upon me.

Now, don't get me wrong. Regret-free living isn't found by continuing to do flawed things, then simply "working through" the regret they cause and moving on. You must also take full responsibility for what you do in the first place—hopefully, before you do them. The more responsibility you take for your choices, the less regret they're likely to cause you. I'm not suggesting a feel-good philosophy that leads people to go untethered to poor decisions and keep on making them. *Responsibility,* a mature concept I did not largely grasp until I was in my twenties, *is a critical step on the road to regret-free living.*

■   ■   ■

I pray this book will help you start to live without debilitating regret and that you will discover that God has amazing things he wants to do with you—things you can't do if you're burdened with regret.

And I hope that you also read with someone else in mind, that you likewise can become a solid support and wise resource for someone filled with their own regrets. You won't have to look far to find such a person.

I'm going to do something I rarely do at the beginning of a book. I'm going to ask you to read these few verses below. There's something in them worth noting at the beginning of this journey.

But the Holy Spirit produces this kind of fruit in our lives: love, joy, peace, patience, kindness, goodness, faithfulness, gentleness, and self-control. There is no law against these things! (Galatians 5:22–23)

What a way to live! With peace and patience rather than impulsive desire for quick fixes or instant relief. With self-control rather than being controlled by an urge, an obsession, or a sin repeated so often it's now an addiction. And look where self-control leads:

Supplement your faith with a generous provision of moral excellence, and moral excellence with knowledge, and knowledge with self-control, and self-control with patient endurance, and patient endurance with godliness, and godliness with brotherly affection, and brotherly affection with love for everyone. (2 Peter 1:5b–7)

Knowing God yields wonderful results, under the guidance and control of the Holy Spirit. This is knowing the God of the universe personally, knowing that his Spirit (and not your ego or fears) compels you. Living like this *does* bring results, and none of them have anything to do with the word *regret*. A regret-filled life is simply not what God wants for you.

If you want the life these verses promise, I think I can help you get there.

CHAPTER 1

Signs of an Unhealthy Relationship

Because of the work I'm blessed to do through New Life Ministries, I witness all kinds of unhealthy relationships all the time. One of the most common characteristics of an unhealthy relationship is two people who continue doing the same things that have never worked for them in the past and can't possibly work for them in the future. Sometimes it's the other person in the relationship who's blowing it, but mostly the individuals I talk with are much like me—people who over the years have had a very active role in perpetuating their own misery.

What people in the misery of unhappy relationships usually fail to realize is that God doesn't *want* them to be miserable. He doesn't want stagnant relationships that aren't going anywhere or are going downward. And the happy truth is that 99 percent of the time, if both people in any unhappy relationship would just be willing to *try* a different way, their misery and stagnation would end. Two people working together in a relationship can overcome just about anything.

Paul says, in 1 Thessalonians 5:16, "Always be joyful." How many of us have been in a relationship that consistently makes us anything *but* joyful? I'm not talking about the bad week all long-term relationships have—or the bad month, or even the bad year. I'm talking about the year-in, year-out drain of a relationship that should have been mended years ago. And if it's a choice or choices *we* have made that have us now stuck in the muck of regrets over a relationship, then it's up to us to find a way out of that mire so we can move on to better choices, better outcomes, a better life.

While there is no formula for fixing every relationship, there are things anyone can do that are sure to bring about the most potential for a healthier future. There *is* a formula for living above and beyond regret, and following it—walking that higher path—is something you can choose to start right now.

Your past ended one second ago, and you begin, *now*, creating a new future for yourself. Joy can be a constant presence in that future.

■　■　■

How do we get stuck in a bad rut in the first place? Well, one of the surest ways is to compare ourselves with the other person and to feel like we are doing more for the good of that relationship. Somehow we build a barrier between ourselves and the other person—and after years in the emotional isolation this creates, it at least feels easier for us to simply continue doing the wrong things we've long been doing than to undertake starting to put things right.

It's like what happens when a bathroom sink begins not to drain as it should. At first you hardly notice the problem. Pretty soon, you see that the water left in the sink after you've brushed your teeth or washed your hands isn't quickly disappearing. Before too long nothing's flowing at all, and you have a problem on your hands.

Now it's only going to be fixed when you stop what you're doing, get out your toolbox, get down on your knees, and start doing what's needed to remove the stinky mess that's preventing the proper flow of things.

The sink-as-relationship metaphor breaks down in one key way, though. Eventually, you do need to fix a clogged sink. But, sadly, a clogged relationship can continue being gunked up forever. Oftentimes it carries on so long its members get blinded to the truth of just how bad their relationship has become. And that's when both people need help regaining their lost perspective.

It's *so* important to be able to recognize a bad relationship when you're in one. That's why I thought it would be a good idea, before we really got into the meat of this book, to take a moment and look at some big road signs that tell you you're traveling down the bad-relationship highway.

All of us have blind spots, areas of ourselves and our lives that we can't, or don't, see. On *New Life Live,* we're helping people see things in and about their relationships that they might have missed. We're helping them understand what principle from God's Word is most applicable in their situation.

But bad relationships don't just surface on the talk show. Each year we produce six New Life Weekends. These are thirty-six-hour, Friday-through-Sunday experiences in six different national locations. People fly in, we bring in clinicians from all over, and we engage and get involved in real lives. We love watching hundreds of people go to work with group counselors and with like-minded fellow strugglers to come out on the other side with new hope and new tools to move forward. In all my years of ministry, I've never been part of anything so powerful. And the results for most everyone are lasting.

One of my favorite couples from our healing weekends had just about come to the end of options for healing their marriage. The husband was there because his wife, as he put it, had "dragged" him. Throughout the course of the weekend, this couple had experienced some insights about themselves and their relationship, but not many.

All this changed in the final hours. In one session the other seven men present, who were being extremely honest with each other, confronted this man about how shabbily he treated his wife. They said he was dismissive toward her. He may not have known much about counseling, but he sure did know the meaning of the word *dismissive*. And it stung his heart to hear from the others how he treated his wife.

He had simply never seen it before. His walking in front of her, his talking past her, his lack of empathy for her . . . it was all from the way he had learned women were to be treated. But once he became aware, for the first time, of how wrong such treatment is, he threw himself into healing his marriage with full dedication and commitment.

Today I can assure you, those two are not living in the darkness of regret. They have started over, and God continues to work in their lives. And it all began when, for the first time, the man opened his heart to the reality of the negative situation he all along had been creating.

Those who are willing to see reality as it is can change that reality and begin to live a life beyond one defined by regret and remorse.

■ ■ ▓

If you're in a relationship that just doesn't feel right to you—that you find is always leaving you, your partner, or even the people around the two of you feeling bad, anxious, or just plain angry—read the following markers of defective relationships and see how many of them apply to yours. If more than two or three of them do—and you can clearly see that they do—then you'll be well on your way to grasping the areas that need your full attention. You and your partner will thus be already headed down the road of healing.

Resentment

It never fails to amaze me how out of touch some people can be with the resentment they're feeling inside toward someone with whom they're in a toxic relationship, whether it is a co-worker, a parent, or a friend. It can be as clear as a bell to everyone around them that they're angry (and to be fair, they often do have all kinds of excellent reasons to feel resentment and anger), but they themselves frequently seem to have no idea what (or how much of it) they're harboring. It's a terribly unhealthy way to live, yet it's the way many people continue to choose to live: full of resentment on the inside but acting—or trying to act—like nothing's wrong on the outside. That's *never* the right choice.

"Surely resentment destroys the fool," we read in Job 5:2. I wish every person I know had those words on their bumper sticker or stitched and framed on the wall of their office or kitchen. These are powerful words. I've dealt with countless people whose lives have been all wrapped up in the resentment they feel for another person—but it's always *they* who are being damaged.

The reason so many people have such a problem comprehending the toxicity of their own resentment is that resentment seethes at a person's deepest level. It lies festering and slowly roiling away beneath everything its host does, says, and thinks. It's like cancer. It's there, it's killing you, and you sometimes aren't even aware of it until it's a problem far beyond anything you can handle on your own. Resentment is not like the animosity we'll look at below; animosity is alive, acting out something in the here and now.

Resentment, on the other hand, is usually rooted in an event or series of events that happened in the past. It's usually the holdover result of something, either specific or general, that was *supposed* to have been resolved, or for which someone was *supposed* to have been forgiven. But (as it turns out) things weren't forgiven. The person who was to be the forgiver *almost* forgave all, but there was anger left over. Maybe not enough to say anything about; maybe not even enough for him or her to be aware it was even there. But it *was* there—and that leftover, sublimated anger is what, over time, becomes the fuel for burning (or smoldering) resentment.

Animosity

Unfortunately, we all know what animosity looks like in any relationship: ugly. There's nothing pretty about two people being openly hostile toward each other.

Not long ago, I was invited to a dinner party hosted by a couple that everyone believed was as happily married as two people can be. The husband was very successful in his business; he and his beautiful wife had raised two sons who'd given them every reason to be proud.

At first the evening went very well indeed. The husband was charming, telling lots of entertaining stories. He kept us all laughing, feeling comfortable and welcomed. His wife, meanwhile, circulated throughout the gathering, always making sure everyone's glass was full and there were plenty of delicious hors d'oeuvres to go around.

It was during dinner, though—the first time, I noticed, that our two "happy" hosts were together in the same room—that I began to detect a distinct disharmony. At first it was just the tone in which she asked her husband if he liked the soup. Then it was his tone as he made a joke I won't repeat here but was just a little bit embarrassing to her.

Then it was her tone and choice of words—nothing too slanderous or offensive, just a word or two with some very definite teeth embedded in them—as she mentioned something about how much time he spent at his office. And then it was definitely his tone and choice of words as he "joked" about how, when he did come home after his hard workday, it was invariably obvious to him how little time she had spent doing much if anything besides watching their wall-sized TV and eating ice cream. It was subtler than I'm describing, but it was there, and it was obvious.

As clear (and uncomfortable to witness) as active animosity is, it also can come in packages much more difficult to detect. Sometimes, in fact, the way hostility presents itself in our lives can be so subtle we might not recognize it. Haven't you ever seen or been around two people at work—or, quite often, two people in the same family—who are forever trading barbs? Barbs never interspersed with any kind words or any genuine affection? And you know how, after about ten minutes around them, your whole jaw starts to ache because you're holding so much tension in it? That's how you know you're around two people who might not be saying right out loud that there's mutual hostility but who nonetheless are plainly conveying it.

If you have any such "always joking" relationships in your own life—and certainly if you regularly find yourself enmeshed in an exchange like the one between that husband and wife during their dinner party—then that's animosity in your life and *you can get rid of it, once and for all.* It's a defect, a very serious problem that no one should allow to go untreated.

Secrecy

I've never known a surer sign that someone is in real trouble than if he's keeping secrets. The wife who's keeping her affair secret from her husband; the son who's keeping his substance abuse secret from his parents; the employee who's keeping secret the office supplies she occasionally takes home from the company supply closet. All such deceptions inevitably destroy intimacy and connection; they lay the foundation for alienation and disconnection.

Secrets are about keeping from someone what they deserve to know. Secrets are about being involved in having people believe something that isn't true. *Secrets are bad.* There's no clearer way to say it. When secrets are founded on deception, they hurt the people the lie is hidden from, and they hurt the secret-keeper even more.

When a mother says to a child about that night's dinner, "It's a secret," she means that it's to be a "surprise" more than a "secret." Sometimes we use the word *secret* in ways that don't involve distorting the truth, or leading others to believe something is true when it isn't, or keeping the truth from those who have a right to know it. That's not what I'm talking about here.

No good can ever come from keeping the real kind of *secret*; the reason someone keeps it in the first place is that they've done something they're ashamed of and are trying to hide it. But keeping a secret about something wrong doesn't make the fact of doing it go away. It doesn't smooth over *or* resolve whatever they did. It can't. Virtually all a secret does is help the concealed lie grow stronger. It's like a mushroom buried in dark, dank, stinky mulch. *All* it can do in that mulch is grow.

Have you ever noticed that whenever you've tried to keep a secret, the pull of "that thing" upon you only grows stronger? If you hide candy under your pillow and throughout the day sneak back into your room for a bite, you're never going to find yourself wanting to do so less often. That's just not the way it works. The longer you keep that secret stash, the more often you're going to find yourself stealing another bite. Pretty soon, you'll be gobbling down two candy bars. Then three. Then four. Before you know it, you'll never leave your bedroom at all, unless it's finally by a crane lifting you through the roof. That's when you'll know it's finally time to seek the help you've needed all along.

Okay, maybe it won't take a whole crane. Maybe it'll just be a bathroom scale or a visit to the dentist. But you get the idea. Secrets make the subject of a secret more potent and alluring than ever.

One of my favorite psalms contains a lot of the most important truths about the harmful effects of secret-keeping:

O Lord, you have examined my heart
and know everything about me.
You know when I sit down or stand up.
You know my thoughts even when I'm far away. . . .
You know everything I do.
You know what I am going to say
even before I say it, Lord. . . .
I could ask the darkness to hide me
and the light around me to become night—
but even in darkness I cannot hide from you.
(Psalm 139:1–4, 11–12a)

Can't get it any clearer than that. You might be able to keep a secret from someone who matters in your life, but you can't keep a secret from the one who matters most (now and in the eternal future): the all-knowing God Almighty.

One of the easiest ways to tell whether you're responsible for what's going wrong in a relationship is to get honest with at least yourself about whether you're harboring any secrets from the other person. If you are, then you don't need to know anything else about the role you're playing in your own misery. As stated above, one of the main reasons we keep secrets is shame about something we did; we think that the fewer people who know about our awful disgrace, the less shame we'll have to experience. But the not-so-funny truth is that no one *ever* judges us as harshly as we judge ourselves. Hiding what you've done doesn't give it less power but, instead, a great deal more.

Perhaps for you the double life of secrecy has itself become a way of life. If so, you may feel alone and isolated, unaware of another way to live. When hidden regrets are brought out in the open, they lose their power, and you make a statement with your life that you truly trust in God, no longer needing to be in control.

If you've dragged a few secrets into your relationship, please know: From here on out, you don't have to create any new ones to keep. A while back, an ex-girlfriend of mine e-mailed our call center saying she wanted to contact me. So I instantly replied—and copied my wife on the exchange. There was never any question in my mind about whether my wife should know about either the e-mail or my response. But there was a time when making that simple decision might not have been so easy for me. I might instead have opted to enjoy a "harmless little secret."

Thank God I know now what I didn't now then: There's no such thing as a secret that's little or harmless.

A secret-filled relationship will be full of regret, missed opportunities, and isolation. The courage to confess, bring into the light, and openly share one's hidden fears or shameful ways is the sure path to freedom. Living without secrets is falling back into God's arms in total, complete trust, free from the need to control or hide. It's certainly worth the effort to at least experiment with (1) growing less and less secretive and (2) being more and more willing to be honest with yourself and others. You can begin living in God's light rather than darkness of your own making!

Power Jockeying

I doubt I knew the term "sibling rivalry" until my late teens, but I lived in the thick of it growing up with two brothers. We were not close; it felt as if we were living three parallel lives that intersected at mealtimes. We fought for attention, fought to look the best, and fought to put each other down. Any two of us made Jacob and Esau look like rookies.

I remember one brother trading me a cherry cough drop for my beloved little black stuffed dog, creatively named Blacky. I can remember the other beating me with a tennis racket after I made some comment about his need to look perfect. (He was a handsome guy and *did* look perfect much of the time.) Each of us wanted the power of attention from our parents and the power of control over each other. Being the youngest, I often won the attention competition, but rarely the control one. So I would leave home with a desire to feel some measure of power in my life.

The pattern from my early days was not easy to change. When someone had power over me—a boss, a teacher, a partner—I found it hard to work beneath them. It stung to the quick when I felt someone was doing something *to* me rather than *with* me.

Since I first started working with broken people back in 1973, I have watched innumerable relationships crumble over the issue of power. I have seen men establish it with bulk and strength. Strange as it may seem, women do the same thing, using size and strength to overpower their children and even sometimes their partners. Overeating and weight gain can also be part of this dynamic, this need to have a powerful presence. Anger, hyper-budgeting, playing the victim, people-pleasing, codependency . . . all these can be used to gain a measure of power.

When relationships move into power-struggle mode, they lose their potential for greatness; only in *shared* power do relationships reach their full promise. Power domination unfolds when a parent doesn't give her love freely and evenly. A husband doles out praise like he's donating blood or giving money to the homeless. A pastor never seems to have anything kind or encouraging to say to any staff member. A supervisor seems to always have her own new favorite employee of the month. A teacher consistently praises the same two or three children in class.

These are the kinds of situations that naturally give rise to power struggles. We've all been there; we all know what it's like to get embroiled in a struggle for dominance. Sometimes we get drawn in so slowly that we barely realize how zealously we've started protecting our own interests. We so gradually become acclimated to our stressful situation that our survival instinct kicks in, and before we know it we are doing everything possible to secure any meager scrap of available power. The parties involved in such a horrid dance have been jigging to the same awful song of rivalry for so long, a lot of their movements have become exceedingly subtle. The fight continues, but over time the punches and stabs have become quicker and harder to see.

Power jockeying can become especially toxic when it comes to define the primary way two people supposedly in a romantic relationship interact with each other. *A relationship based on who's winning all the time is one in which both parties are losing all the time.* Relationships—especially "romantic" ones—are supposed to be based on love and mutual support, not sniping and putting the other person down. But too often people readily lose track of how, just as Jesus will lift up all believers one day, we, his followers, are to lift up others every day.

If you have a relationship you're feeling uncomfortable or stressed about, look carefully at the way you behave toward the other person. See if you spend a lot of time jockeying for power. If they share a story with you, do you immediately jump in or quickly follow with a story that "tops" theirs? If they accomplish or are proud of something, do you join in with their enthusiasm— or do you undercut your congratulations with a subtle reference to something they didn't do or didn't do quite well enough? If they point left, do you point right? Is the thrill you get from the relationship based on winning, or on loving? Know this: If it's in "winning," then you're actually losing.

If "love" more often than not feels like war, then you can be sure you have regrets piling up inside you. This means at some point you will look back and see what could have been, what might have happened, the good relationship you missed out on, just because you felt you needed to be in control of it.

Well, you can change that, right now; you can begin to move out of your power-seeking patterns and enter into a reciprocal relationship where needs other than your need for power are met. In the same way, if you find yourself always being controlled, you likewise can make some moves that will change the dynamics of your difficult relationship.

Whether we're prone to exert it over others or tend to allow someone else to hold it over us, power need not drive a relationship. With God's help, it is possible to transform earthly power into godly love.

Unresolved Problems

One *New Life Live* listener called to talk about the problem she was having with her husband. She'd discovered he was hiding money from her. She'd been in his office, going through the desk drawers (something that almost never turns up anything good), when she found, hidden underneath some folders, a checkbook she'd never seen before.

She opened it and saw that for at least a year he'd been keeping another checking account. There wasn't a lot of money involved, and from what she could see he wasn't writing checks to a house of ill repute or a bookie or anything along those lines. In fact, many had been written to the same kind of daily-use businesses (like dry cleaners and grocery stores) that she herself used all the time—but it upset her nonetheless to have discovered that her husband was keeping such a secret.

Sensing that there was more to her story about their relationship than she was revealing or was maybe even aware of, I asked this woman to calm down a bit and talk more about what was going on in her house. What I really wanted to know about was how her and her husband's intimate life was going; often the state of a marriage is reflected by what's happening in the marital bedchambers.

She wasn't opening up, though, so I decided to just come right out and ask.

"Oh, that," she said dismissively. "He prefers not to sleep in our bedroom anymore. For about the last month or two, he's been sleeping in a bed he set up in his office." And then she went on to say how she was wondering whether it would be a good idea for her to hire a private detective to track down everyone to whom her husband had written a check out of his private, hidden account.

"Whoa, whoa," I said. "Hold on a minute. Did you just say that for one or two months your husband has been sleeping in a bed in his office? He actually set up a whole separate bedroom for himself, and that's where he's sleeping now?"

"Yes, that's right." She said it in a tone that indicated she really did think (or was determined to act like she thought) that her husband's no longer sleeping in her bed was no more remarkable than if he had developed a sudden interest in avocado growing or in model trains.

At the beginning of my counseling career, it would have surprised me that this woman could act like this was an incidental relational detail. But over the years, time and time again, I've seen how people would rather concentrate on the hole in the sail than on the hole in the bottom of the boat. Knee deep in water, already below the surface, they'll still be looking up at that little puncture in the sail.

"That's why we're not going anywhere," they'll say as they sink deeper and deeper into the sea.

Pay attention to unresolved conflicts in your life. And I don't mean the kind of long-established resentments mentioned earlier. Here I mean issues that are hot, are current, and have import today. You can't just ignore unaddressed conflicts and hope they'll go away. There's almost no guarantee more certain that regret is in your future than if you're not directly confronting a current significant relational problem.

Unhealthy Alliances

"Tell me what company you keep and I'll tell you what you are." These words are as true now as they were when penned in the sixteenth century (by the Spanish writer Miguel de Cervantes). Whether or not we want to be, we're known by the company we keep.

Most of us want to be the kind of guy or gal people of quality care to associate with. The problem is, people of quality tend to want to associate with those who are healthy, adjusted, successful, and good-natured. It's hard to be those things when you're filled with anger and regret. When bitterness and resentment have taken over an important relationship, or when you're constantly piling shame on yourself for something wrong you did, then you're probably not spending a lot of time being the sort of person that quality folks prefer.

One of the most helpful things a person can do by way of assessing the quality of their personal lives is to take a careful inventory of those with whom they regularly associate. When you look around at the ones you've surrounded yourself with, do you see people you're proud to be associated with?

Are they helping you heal from and *avoid* regret, or do you know deep inside they're more likely than not to one day *cause* you regret?

Be careful to ensure that no matter how ugly things get between you and someone you're in relationship with, resist keeping company with those who merely feed off the negative emotions of others. We all know people who treasure that fuel. People attracted to others' trouble or drama like vultures are drawn to roadkill. People who seem to get up when you're down, always just a little *too* interested in your latest conflict, slight, or failure.

There's always that one person in the office who's first at the water cooler with the latest gossip. That one kid who rushes ahead of the others to tell a teacher or parent about something bad that happened. That one friend who starts calling or visiting more than usual, for the wrong reasons, whenever you're going through a rough personal time.

Even worse than bad-weather folks are those who are forever volunteering (somehow, aggressively) to "help" you deal with whomever you're struggling with. They're forever egging you on to write that nasty letter, go through with that heated confrontation, send that accusatory e-mail, make that angry phone call. They usually aren't interested in helping you resolve your conflicts—everything getting better wouldn't be any fun for them at all. They want to pretend to be your friend by sitting you down on your little stool back in your corner, toweling you off, spraying some water into your mouth, giving you a little pep talk, then sending you back out there so you can make war and get bloodied again.

If you see one too many negative people (and one is one too many) in your life, determine if they're a peripheral player or one of the main players. If they're "primary," then you've got some work to do getting to the bottom of your real problem with him or her. If they're a secondary character—a co-worker, an acquaintance, someone who knows someone who knows someone who knows you—consider cutting them out of your life altogether. People drawn to regret-producing dynamics almost always, sooner or later, themselves become a cause for regret.

> *Walk with the wise and become wise;*
> *associate with fools and get in trouble.* (Proverbs 13:20)

Putting Yourself First

I almost wish I didn't know as much as I do about how putting self first can lead to regrets. (Sadly, it's having done so much of this that qualifies me as capable of writing a book on avoiding regret.) At somewhere around age fifty, I began to see my life in a different light—in the light of truth rather than the light of deception. I realized that the biggest portion of my responsibility for my trouble and pain was that I too often chose to put myself ahead of my family—all in the name, of course, of ministry and doing God's work.

I was developing and nurturing a daily-growing ministry. Every time I turned around, someone else wanted my advice, my energy, my time, my thoughts, my love. And I gave and gave and gave of those resources until finally I had given too much. I became a casualty of too much travel, too many commitments, too many opportunities. Nothing I did was in and of itself especially bad or destructive; it was the cumulative toll that was too much for those I loved and for me to bear.

You might say, "But, Steve, that doesn't sound to me like you were putting yourself first. It sounds like you were putting other people ahead of you." And it's true that to a considerable degree that's exactly what was happening. Yet there's another side to being the sort of person who is always putting others first. It has taken me a lot of years, innumerable hours of honest introspection, dedicated listening to the wisdom of those around me, and an ongoing desire to know the truth and to know Jesus to arrive where I'm at today. If I know anything, I know that it's dangerously easy to confuse doing for others with doing for self.

This is where that evil old devil, the ego, comes slithering in. If I'm giving another person material or spiritual assistance, there's no doubt (I hope) that it's genuinely helping. But what's also undeniably true is that it's helping *me*, making me feel wonderful about myself. My actions all along were beneficial to others; if I'm honest about it, though, I have to admit that as often as not my true motive for helping others was often to comfort or reassure *me*. Anytime someone was benefiting from my largess, my wisdom, my generosity, I was feeling intelligent, competent, and caring. It really was all about me. Not on the surface, but way down deep. And that "deep" ultimately pulled me down into doing too much, too often, for too many.

It's just that easy—as easy as it is to think "I'm great!"—to turn a gift from God into something damaging.

> *Watch out! Don't do your good deeds publicly, to be admired by others, for you will lose the reward from your Father in heaven. When you give to someone in need, don't do as the hypocrites do— blowing trumpets in the synagogues and streets to call attention to their acts of charity! I tell you the truth, they have received all the reward they will ever get. But when you give to someone in need, don't let your left hand know what your right hand is doing. Give your gifts in private, and your Father, who sees everything, will reward you.* (Matthew 6:1–4)

Now's the time to think about your own life and see to what extent—and especially how subtly—you too often put yourself first. It's easy enough to do under any circumstances, but it's particularly tempting when you're embroiled in a difficult relationship. If you're always angling for what's best for you, always trying to arrange things so that they come out best for number one, you need to change that. While putting yourself first might sometimes gain for you a temporary advantage, it's God's law that in the end such a life strategy will only leave you filled with regrets.

Defective but Regret-Free

Most likely you've heard the adage that it's not what happens to us that's important, but rather how we react to it. I believe this to be one of life's greatest truths. We often approach life hoping and wishing nothing bad will happen to us, and then, when it does, we respond poorly. If we know crummy things *are* going to happen, expecting them and being ready for them when they do happen, then we're better equipped to respond to unhealthy stuff in healthy ways.

If your response to hurt is shock, and out of fear or anger you try to hurt back whoever hurt you, then you're adding greatly to your own regret pile. But if you know that God wants to use your pain to heal you and build you, you can absorb the initial blow. You're also better able to prevent whatever happened from becoming a pattern in your life.

Perhaps right now you're in a place where, goodness knows, I have often enough found myself. Perhaps you're full of pain and regret. Maybe you're in a situation that no one but you got yourself into. You feel stupid, alone, and abandoned, and you are wondering if God is really there for you. You may feel you have to find your way, figure it out, try really hard this time, and pull yourself out of the mess.

But that is *not* the way toward a regret-free path, which is one determined by a conviction that God cares. That's all you have to believe. Trust that God is full of love—*is* love—and that no matter the wilderness we find ourselves traveling in, he's there, ready to guide us to goodness.

So let me take a moment here to proclaim an absolute truth about regret-free living. You can't experience it without putting your hope and trust in God. You must admit where you are, then ask God to do with you what only God can. Turn over your self-pity and pain and begin to focus on what you can do today, while at the same time believing that God will do the miraculous in your life over the years still ahead.

If you do this—if you live by these simple truths—then a strange dynamic will overtake you on your journey. You will find that some of the worst things become some of the best things. Bitterness becomes gratitude; anger, love; aggression, acceptance.

Above all, you find yourself—after a life of hurts, pains, traps, mistakes, and trouble—living through it all, and beyond, without regret. I hope you want this enough to walk through some tough things to get there.

■　■　■

One final note before we leave these elements that mark a regret-bound relationship. This past Halloween, my family escorted my youngest son, Solomon, as he went door to door. (We just see Halloween as a time when our kids get dressed up in non-evil-looking costumes and have some fun. Plus, I love looking around people's homes, and this is a way to kind of get a nosy tour of the neighborhood.)

Solomon was dressed as Elmo, and in his hand he carried what looked like the plastic-bucket head of another Elmo. Along with me dressed as a clown—red hair, red nose, and red hearts on long underwear under red shorts—he set out with the rest of the family.

Along the way, Solomon didn't eat too much of his fairly gotten gain. When we got home, he put the bucket on the table and began to point.

"Can I eat this one?" he said.

I said yes.

"Can I eat this one?"

Again, I said yes.

"Can I eat this one?"

He could—and he did.

But that was the last one I allowed him to eat at the time.

I love that boy. And I wanted him to have some fun, and I wanted him to have a little candy. But I don't want him to have more candy than is good for him.

I immediately related this to God's will for us. There are many choices we can make for ourselves at any given time that are perfectly fine with God. And God wants to say yes to us about a lot of the good things we want for ourselves. But a lot of bad things out there, tempting us to choose them, are dreadful for us—things we think we want for ourselves, choices that in the moment we'd very much like to make. Sometimes—just like Solomon had to do with me, his earthly father—we have to put ourselves under our Father's authority and trust that he only wants us to have what, in the long run, is really and truly best for us.

Then we have to make his choices—we have to have the *strength* to make his choices—our own. And we gather that strength piece by piece, step by step, one sweet and right little choice at a time.

CHAPTER 2

Admitting the State of Affairs

I know it's not a very pleasant request, but I want you to imagine for a moment that you just saw a silverfish. You know what silverfish are, right? They're flat little bugs with long, wavy antennae that scurry around in a wriggling, fishlike way. The ones that always disappear into a dark crack at the very moment you're about to squish it. (Some scholars say silverfish have been around since at least the Paleozoic Era. Does that make you feel any better about them? Me either.)

So let's say you saw a silverfish in your garage or under your sink (they like moist areas), and you didn't think much of it. After all, it's just one bug, right? How much harm can it do, anyway?

Then, let's say a week or so later, you saw another one. No problem; again, it's just one bug—maybe even the same bug you'd already seen (they all look alike) and just missed squishing.

And then, let's say after another week, you see *another* silverfish. This one's a baby. It's a silverfish-ette.

Now, how long do you think you'll be able to go before you face the fact that you have a full-blown infestation? A month? A half year? A full year? Two? It's amazing how long some people can avoid facing the bugs living in their house. I once knew a dear woman whose home was so filled with cockroaches that whenever she switched on her kitchen lights, she would stand still for a moment or two, listening to the rattling hiss of a thousand cockroaches scurrying for cover.

This was not a crazy or filthy woman by any means. It's just that her bug problem had reached such a state over such a long period that by the time their number would make the average person scream, she barely counted them as an inconvenience. To her, they'd slowly but surely become just an everyday part of her life.

Although it's unlikely that you think so, you might be the same way about your "bug" problem. After all, silverfish are quiet. They don't bite people. (They like starch and sugar!) And like cockroaches, they're wholly nocturnal. It's easy enough to close your eyes at night and pretend the issue just doesn't exist.

Yet it does. It's there. And sooner or later you'll need to do something about it.

It's the same way with the kind of relationship problems that ultimately lead to regret. The problems you're having with your boss, friend, spouse, or child might seem small enough now. They might stay mostly underground; they might remain mostly hidden from sight. They might only take the smallest occasional bite out of you—at the time you might barely feel it at all.

But again, the problems are there, real and growing. And if you don't admit the evidence you have—if you continue to ignore them—then, as sure as silverfish love book glue (sugar *and* starch), your relationship problems will proliferate and grow into large, creepy things that'll make you regret not handling them sooner.

Doing an Honest, Fearless Assessment

The reason so many people seem willing to simply carry on with dysfunctional relationships rather than stop and try to fix whatever is wrong is grounded in a word we just ran right by: *stop.*

If you're going to take control of a bad relationship that seems to have taken control of you, one thing you're going to have to do— and maybe the most difficult thing—is really and truly stop.

I want to confess right now that I am one of the world's worst stoppers. I don't even like to stop for red lights. Of course, I do, because I hate even more having to stop when I see red and blue lights blinking off the top of the squad car behind me. But stopping still comes extremely unnaturally for me. What I'm very good at is going-going-going like the Energizer Bunny. To me, there's always something ahead that's interesting, always something around the next turn I'm dying to see. In my world, it's what's next that's best.

One of the reasons I've had difficulty stopping in the past is that relationships were uncomfortable for me. So instead of using them to connect with others, I just kept myself moving forward to the next thing. What I failed to realize is that, while I was so fixated on what was next, what was happening right in front of me was not getting anywhere near enough attention. I had a family who needed me to be more interested in them than in anything else in this whole world. But I wasn't being to them the person I should have been; I thought they were okay without me. I minimized their needs and believed they were doing just fine as "we" tried to help people all over the globe with their struggles. I was a lot of things in those days, but I wasn't the husband, partner, father, coach, encourager, and friend my family needed. I was too busy being dazzled by what was ahead of me to see what was before me.

It took a long time, but finally the situation I'd been creating all crashed down upon me. The collapse of the married life I'd known was so painful that I didn't know if I could work through it; I didn't, in fact, know if there even was life on the other side of it. There was, thankfully, and I am living on the other side of that pain, grateful for what I have learned and wanting to help others avoid some of my blunders.

If you want to avoid some of my biggest life errors, make sure you don't neglect any important relationship in your life, no matter how "wonderful" the other things you're doing. And the way to do that is to make certain that before the inevitable relationship crash, you take the time to *stop*. Stopping is the first step on the road to preventing regret. If you're experiencing stress or dysfunction in any important relationship—or are feeling just fine, but the folks around you are feeling the stress and pain you're causing—then you need to make yourself stop.

The reason is simple. You need to think, contemplate, and reflect. And you can't do that if you're moving, if you're collecting incoming information, if you're still out there furiously playing the game from which you know, in your heart of hearts, it's time to take a break.

You can't get an overview of something you're not really looking at. And what you need to do with any bad relationship is to very definitely, very carefully look at it. *Look at it thoroughly. Look at it honestly.*

Whenever we take a test of the sort we took in school, we stop for a moment and bring into the present all the pertinent knowledge and understanding we've collected in the past. We take what we know and have learned and formulate it in such a way that in the present it makes sense, it's applicable, it stands the test of scrutiny and evaluation.

We *objectify* our knowledge and experience.

It's the same with our relationships. Every once in a while, instead of simply living day by day, we've got to step back to honestly, thoroughly evaluate. Instead of being so wrapped up in what an important primary relationship is becoming, we have to concern ourselves with what it actually, presently is.

The best way to do that—the best way to get the best view of any relationship—is to stop, step back, and ask God to help us see what we're too small, weak, and purposefully busy to grasp ourselves. Our human perspective can't begin to compare with what God can show us.

In a lot of ways, the show of our life can only *start* when we stop, sit down, and start truly looking at it.

Proverbs 3:5–7 issues this challenge:

Lean not on your own understanding. . . .
  Do not be wise in your own eyes. (NIV)

Then, in 12:15:

Fools think their own way is right,
  but the wise listen to others.

So besides stopping to be aware and evaluating, we must also reach outside ourselves to get needed feedback about our experience—our reality. Sometimes, doing that can be even tougher than stopping.

Asking for the Other's Input and Opinion

Have you ever been so wrapped up you could barely think amid the emotional turmoil that comes from knowing something has gone terribly wrong with an important relationship? It's just a plain ol' awful feeling. Something that's gone sour can make it so you can't sleep; sometimes (although for me only when things have gotten really bad) you can't eat.

When there's something badly wrong where you wish you had a great relationship, it can dominate your every waking thought. While you're driving, cooking, or filling out paper work, your mind, on its own, is worrying over everything you said or did and everything he or she said or did to you. Were they justified when they said that one thing? Was there a perfectly good reason for you to have done what you did? If the case had gone to trial, what would your lawyer present to the judge? What evidence would show you to be in the wrong? And what would be the verdict? Who's right? It's like a puzzle your mind just won't leave alone until it's solved.

All of this is doubly true if your relationship has left you with feelings of regret. Knowing you were wrong—or even just sensing that you were probably wrong—can become like quicksand you've tripped and fallen into. It can feel like there's no way of breaking free of that heavy, sinking feeling. And struggling—fighting it by waving your arms, kicking and screaming—only pulls you down deeper and deeper.

Yet most people still would rather let the quicksand of regret bury them than take the steps necessary to get back onto solid land.

They just don't want to face regret. They'd rather go on with the fact that they were wrong tucked somewhere into their mind than pull that fact into the front of their mind, where they could give it the attention that sooner or later it's going to demand anyway.

That's a shame, because the first, best, and most direct thing you can do whenever you're feeling uneasy or regretful about the state of your relationship is so simple a child would think of it. *To get a relationship out of the pits, talk with the other person.*

That's it. Just talk. Not at them, but with them. How many problems would be resolved, how many misunderstandings would be cleared up, how much stress in the world would be avoided if people who were having mutual difficulties would just *talk* together?

What's amazing about this widespread reticence is that everyone knows talking almost always helps two antagonistic people peacefully move toward each other. How many shared problems have you had that weren't significantly improved once conversation between the two of you was initiated? Isn't it true that in the course of such a conversation, you learn a perspective on the problem that you hadn't seen before, or are made aware of some fact bearing on the circumstances that you didn't know about, or hadn't considered, until your attention was drawn to it?

If you're feeling regret about something you did or said to someone, please talk with that person. Tell them you're feeling bad. Let them do for you what people really enjoy doing for others: relieving someone of regret.

As you converse with him or her, chances are great you'll come away feeling infinitely lighter. Ask the person to tell you truthfully what they saw in you that was disappointing or inconsistent. Tell them you want their input; let them know you are sincere about wanting to make things right. Most likely the two of you will end up closer. Ultimately, you may even replace the regret of what happened between the two of you with gratitude for its having brought you nearer together.

Seeking Input From Friends

In the final stretch of the 2008 presidential election, I saw something so amazing it took me a couple of moments to believe what I was seeing. During one network's election coverage, one of the two political analysts standing together talking face-to-face wasn't even in the studio. She was a full-sized, perfectly clear holographic projection! She looked like Princess Leia when R2-D2 cast her 3-D image before a startled Luke Skywalker. At that moment viewers were wearing on their faces Luke's same expression: stunned and awed.

After the two commentators were done discussing, the holographic woman explained she was really located miles and miles away from the studio, inside a special tent set up for the sole purpose of producing the results we were then witnessing. She was surrounded by a bunch of cameras, each catching her from a slightly different angle. When all the images were (somehow) blended into one and then broadcast back to the studio, the result was the 3-D projection appearing on my TV. It was incredible. (And I'm afraid we just exhausted my understanding of how that all worked. It was lucky for me that I even figured out how to get my TV turned on in the first place.)

Sometimes we're needing to fully understand something we've done wrong, or seeking to gain clarity on a negative effect we've had on someone else. Sometimes we're trying to figure out what we did or said that led us to suffer profound regret. When this happens, we need to see ourselves through the angle and lenses of others. Just as that reporter had different cameras surrounding her, with each one seeing her just a little differently, so sometimes we need to ask others who know us, or who were around us when the trouble happened, what they saw.

And if we ask enough people what they saw and experienced—their individual perspective on us at that time—very often we can put together a well-rounded, fuller version of ourselves than we could ever hope to get simply by looking at ourselves, by ourselves. With others' help and input, we can see more of who we are and who we've been than with only a limited, flat, one-dimensional self-view.

We too can go 3-D!

After one of several times in my life when I felt terribly betrayed by someone, I had to steel myself for what I might hear—and then go around, one by one, to the many friends I'd acquired over the years to ask for their perspective on (1) what went wrong with my relationship and (2) what I could or even should do about it. I knew I might have to hear some things that would hurt—and boy, did I ever. But as much as it hurt, asking those friends for their perspective was one of my life's most valuable and rewarding experiences. It's how I learned to finally come to terms with so much heartache that (surprise!) I had caused.

■ ■ ■

Let me leave this section on the importance of trusted counsel with words from Proverbs. I hope they'll help you as much as they did me.

Wounds from a sincere friend
are better than many kisses from an enemy. . . .
The heartfelt counsel of a friend
is as sweet as perfume and incense. (27:6, 9)

Surveying the Relationship's History

Poet Maya Angelou once wrote, "History, despite its wrenching pain, cannot be unlived, but if faced with courage, need not be lived again." These inspirational words should be read over and over by anyone who feels they can never move from the dark regret of their past into the bright hope of their future.

Sure, you've done wrong. And there's no way around the fact that you're going to have to pull that past into your present and deal with it. You'll need to put balm on those wounds, wrap those old sores, and tend to the pain you've caused. But in so doing you can also shed the regret you once earned. *Living with regret is not a life sentence.* It's like anything you have to pay the price for—you can pay it and move on.

One of the prices you have to pay for a life free of oppressive regret is a thorough and brutally honest survey of the entire history of whatever relationship is troubling your soul. Even though it's what delivers our pain into our present life, we are too quick to forget the past. It's too easy to take general complacency about who we are now and project it backward into the past. Herein, everywhere we look at ourselves in the past, we see someone (especially if we don't look too closely) we're not at all ashamed to have been.

If you look back on your past and don't find someone who should accept the blame for the regret you're feeling now—who is culpable for whatever went wrong back then—then you're not looking back at your past with nearly enough honesty and integrity.

You're still trying to fake yourself out, which means you're destined to continue tripping over your own feet. The chances are excellent that whatever happened that's darkening your door today was bad and wrong; trying to pretend it wasn't—that you were just the victim of circumstances, or were doing the best you could—is only going to make the shadows around you grow bigger and darker.

What allows us to step into the future is stepping back into the past. If a relationship has gone wrong—leaving you or the other person resentful or remorseful—then it's your responsibility to take a long, hard, clear-eyed look at the relationship's history. *All of it,* not just the parts that somehow make you look good or involve you getting hurt and "naturally" reacting in whatever negative way.

This is about carefully and thoroughly assessing the entirety of the history between you. You'll need to remember more than just the real-time, actual events. You also must reflect upon the emotional realities of what was going on with that relationship at a given time. You'll have to admit a truth that's most difficult for any of us to acknowledge: Other people's experience and version of what occurred are just as valid as ours. We're not usually open to fully appreciating this. We usually want our "reality" to be the biggest, truest, and most important.

And we can have this, if we want. We can insist that's the case, that ultimately what happened to us is all that *really* matters. We can keep telling ourselves this. But God, who knows and sees all, knows better.

You are God's beloved creation—and so is the other person to or with whom, in whatever measure, you did wrong.

Want to please God? Then go back over the history that's causing you regret and honestly face every single moment of it. We'll examine how to do so with love, in a humble state of mind, and aware that only God's forgiveness can ever cleanse you of your transgressions.

In the end, the only way to claim your future is to claim your past.

Dare to Reach a Firm and Clear Conclusion

Envision living in a rural Indian village, a hundred years ago. And imagine that there have been tiger attacks on the outskirts. Nothing too gory—no one's actually been eaten or even maimed— but the livestock of farmers have been, and the villagers have glimpsed and even been chased by the hungry tiger increasingly prowling the edges of town.

Imagine that because of the tiger all village life has come to a standstill. People are afraid to go out at night. During the day, no one wants to wander too far. No one will fetch water alone. People spend less time in their fields, fearing that if they doze beneath a tree or linger much in the open, they'll be attacked and eaten. Mothers won't let their children play outside. Everyone is living in fear of the fearsome beast.

Imagine that you decide enough is enough, that you're going to be the one to hunt down and kill the tiger that has ruined the lives of your family and friends. You grab your trusty arms, kiss your spouse good-bye, hug your children for what you at least hope won't be the last time, step outside your house, and head for the wilds beyond the village.

Now, what do you do once you get out there? You hunt the tiger, right? You don't start wandering around aimlessly. You don't forget what you're doing, drop your weapon, and become lost in the beauty of a plant. You don't hear water running somewhere and dreamily make your way through the thicket to a river, sitting for an hour or two, peacefully watching the water go by.

No. You concentrate. You focus. You look for the signs of where the tiger has been, and you follow them, and you keep following them until you find the animal that's so dramatically changed life for the worst.

And then, having tracked down the cause of your discontent, you do what you have to do.

You make the tiger chase you around and around a tree very fast, until finally he turns himself into butter. Then you have some delicious pancakes, and everyone lives happily ever after.

I'm kidding.

You take care of business. You do what you came there to do.

It's the same way with tracking down and discovering the cause (or causes) of your regret. Regret hounding you is like our village-hounding tiger. Your regret is out there, lurking in the shadows just beyond your normal life; it's watching and stalking you; it's keeping you from enjoying being alive. The only way it's ever going to stop compromising the quality of your life is if you finally decide to do something about it, arm yourself with wisdom and courage, march toward where you know the monster is lurking, track it down, and eliminate it.

You can't eliminate a tiger without a weapon. What's a crucial weapon for eliminating regret? Clarity of thought, that's what. More specifically, to eliminate the prowling tiger of regret, you must find a very firm, very clear conclusion about what it is, exactly, that led to your regret in the first place.

If you go back to discover your regret's origin and you find that, say, you spoke more harshly than you should have, then boom—that's your conclusion. Stay there. Believe in it. Let it tell you what you're to do next.

If, when your child needed you, you disappointed him or her, then boom—there you have it. That's what happened. No need to distill, distort, or deflect. Call it what it is. Plant your flag of truth upon it and claim it as yours, yours alone.

Maybe you acted like a coward. Maybe you shirked your responsibility. Maybe you were arrogant or dismissive. Maybe you're feeling regret that you shouldn't; maybe you've been too quick to assume responsibility for something that's really someone else's fault.

Jesus said, "You are truly my disciples if you remain faithful to my teachings. And you will know the truth, and the truth will set you free" (John 8:31–32). So make it your business to track down, name, and claim the truth of whatever it is you've done that's now causing you regret. Don't just know it. Change the way you live because of it. Without doing that, the shackles of your regret certainly will continue to bind and hold you fast.

CHAPTER 3

Acknowledging Your Responsibility

I once knew a man who kept so busy winning conflicts with different colleagues that he didn't realize he may have been winning some battles but was definitely losing the war. Everyone around him realized that if he kept behaving the same way, he was going to end up unemployed. And it wouldn't have been the first time he'd argued and fought his way right out a job's front door. His résumé was a history of places filled with people who (for reasons he could go on and on about) stubbornly refused to acknowledge his genius, and they were all idiots.

At the time I met this very qualified and unarguably talented man, he was on the verge of losing yet another high-paying, high-powered job. While he understood that yet again something was going terribly wrong, his mind stopped short whenever it arrived at the part of the story where it would make sense to begin holding himself accountable for at least some of what wasn't working.

One day, after enduring yet another long litany of atrocities visited upon him by the uncaring and unknowing people where he worked, I gently suggested he consider the possibility that the turmoil had less to do with others than with him.

How he *railed* against the thought! *He* was right; *everyone* else was wrong; the very idea that there might be any other truth at work in his life was like suggesting the sun is actually the moon.

As I listened to his indignant protestations, 2 Corinthians 5:10 popped into my mind.

"Friend," I said, "Paul says, 'We must all stand before Christ to be judged. We will each receive whatever we deserve for the good or evil we have done in this earthly body.' You might want to reflect upon this."

His first response was an expression of consternation. Then he looked confused—and then pensive. Shortly thereafter he cut our meeting short and headed for the door.

Two days later he called, asking if we could get together for lunch.

There's a look people get—a peaceful, humble glow that seems to radiate from their core—when they've had a direct learning encounter with Jesus. That's what had happened to this man. The Holy Spirit within him had been awakened, turning a lion into a lamb.

"You were dead right," he said, to my astonishment. "I was causing the very situations that were giving me such grief. I hadn't even seen it." He went on to share how the Lord had seen fit to open his eyes and show him the reality behind the illusions he'd so long chosen to believe.

In this chapter, I want to help you do what this man did— recognize how important it is to take complete responsibility for mistakes made by you, and you alone.

The Challenge of Owning What's Yours

If there's one thing you can say about nearly anyone, it's that they don't want to make mistakes. At the very least, most people, if honest, would have to admit that they long to be thought of as a person whom others would like to resemble. All human beings are driven to be better—no matter how they personally might define that—than they are. Wanting to be more later than you are now is part of life's natural ambition.

Ultimately, what we *most* want to be is beyond reproach. While the desire for such imperviousness is very human indeed, Christians are perhaps especially inclined to desire it. God's children can feel driven to try to seem as if they never misbehave, taking very seriously the idea that they're to be as godlike as they can possibly will themselves to be.

> All of us who have had that veil [of unbelief] removed can see and reflect the glory of the Lord. And the Lord—who is the Spirit— makes us more and more like him as we are changed into his glorious image. (2 Corinthians 3:18)

> God knew his people in advance, and he chose them to become like his Son, so that his Son would be the firstborn among many brothers and sisters. (Romans 8:29)

The Lord makes us more and more like him! We are to be changed into his glorious image! We've been chosen to be like Jesus!

No wonder we all sit up straight in church. That's a pretty tall order.

And it's one we can fulfill too; the Lord assures us of that. But what we must do is seek to emulate him through the Spirit's transformative powers—not, as so many of us do, put all our hope in becoming more Christlike on the exercise of our weak, imperfect human will.

"Pride goes before destruction, and haughtiness before a fall" (Proverbs 16:18). People are prideful when trying for self-greatness; they are pleasing to God when they let him make of them what he will.

What inevitably happens when you try to make *yourself* perfect is that, before you can say "Get out of the way—that's mine!" you fail. You say the wrong thing. You act selfishly, or foolishly, or foolishly selfish. Driven by what amounts to nothing more than ego, you invariably behave as if you care for nothing more than yourself. Ultimately, you *do* care for no one or nothing as much as yourself.

In honoring yourself, you dishonor God.

One of the biggest signs that a person has spent or is spending too much time worrying about what's best for them is that they refuse to admit when they've done something wrong. We all know someone who seems constitutionally incapable of understanding that it's just possible they're not God's gift to human perfection. Such people also are sure not going to admit that something they did in the past is wrong. They're too busy looking at their image in the mirror to honestly reflect upon their past.

If you want to get over your regret and shed your shame, you must be able to admit nothing simpler—and nothing more challenging—than that you're human. It's hard to let go of the idea that, in your own way, you're just as flawed as anyone else—that, to us, we're actually *more* flawed, since we know our weaknesses and mistakes most intimately.

Owning what's yours is admitting there's bad stuff *to* be owned. Admitting that you're broken truly is the first step to getting fixed. And *admitting that you can't fix yourself—that only God can—is the first step to staying fixed.*

The Plank in Your Own Eye

"It's obvious to me and others in the organization that there is a leadership problem in our Dallas call center. You either need to be willing to move there, or I will promote someone else to run that operation."

Those words I used began a process that led to the resignation of the most talented, energetic, faithful, bright, hardworking person with whom I have ever had the joy of working. This man never backed away from a challenge. Three hundred thousand women coming to Women of Faith conferences every year was not too big for this guy. He did it all—and I watched him leave the organization.

When I finally took a look backward and inward, this became a source of tremendous regret to me. The fellow was doing so much to help grow the ministry, and because I misjudged a problem and its solution, I lost him to (of all things) an insurance company. At the time, New Life was just getting on its feet. We had tons of enthusiasm, a few successful programs that heralded good things, more plans than we knew what to do with, and—as I soon learned—a management structure more suited to a small catering service than a thriving counseling and radio ministry.

One of the best things New Life had going for it then (and today) were the people who had come into it on the ground floor, dedicated folks who looked at our humble state and saw nothing but what we could become.

One of the sincere, dedicated, and honest people who in those early days chose to hook their stars to what would evolve into New Life was this incredible guy I'll refer to as Curt. Curt was one of my top-level people, basically my second in command. Curt wasn't a large-persona type; he never called attention to himself, never raised his voice, never made decisions in a panic, always patiently listened to what people around him had to say.

Curt also practiced a wonderful management philosophy. He shaped the responsibilities of everyone below him according to their unique gifts and propensities. If someone in accounting was good with concepts but not so hot with follow-the-books procedures, he would slowly but surely move that person to the job that best fit. If another person was good with people, he'd adjust their responsibilities so that before too long they'd be working in personnel or public relations.

Whatever your talent, propensity, or desire, Curt would work with you so that you felt you were being appreciated for who you were: for your special gifts, your special contribution. You would know you were valued at work for who you were, not just for what you could do. Curt made a lot of people feel very good about working for us; this propelled us into fast growth and some very effective ministry.

Unfortunately, I wasn't anywhere near wise enough to understand the value of the way Curt operated. In those days, I was so busy managing in my way (which consisted of way too much pointing, judging, and criticizing). I wanted things to happen now, immediately, yesterday. And my insecure need to see results blinded me to just how valuable Curt was to me and the organization. For one very important thing, he knew how to manage *me*.

Curt, unafraid to be open and honest, was one of those people who would always tell me the truth. He was a levelheaded executive who knew what was needed to get the job done. He warned me of troubles up ahead; he prepared me for difficult tasks coming my way; he did it all with the greatest of attitudes. And I never appreciated it more than after Curt left us. It was a long time before I found the people I work with now. In the interim there was much mediocrity in our workplace—and most of it came from me.

I love it when at key moments bits of applicable Scripture will pop into my head. Long after Curt had left, as I sat thinking about how much I missed him, Matthew 7 came into my heart:

> *You will be treated as you treat others. The standard you use in judging is the standard by which you will be judged.* (v. 2)

And then,

> *Why worry about a speck in your friend's eye when you have a log in your own? How can you think of saying to your friend, "Let me help you get rid of that speck in your eye," when you can't see past the log in your own eye? Hypocrite! First get rid of the log in your own eye; then you will see well enough to deal with the speck in your friend's eye.* (vv. 3–5)

I saw those words in my mind's eye—and I was then moved to make contact with Curt again. I did so, and we became friends. When the time was right, I asked Curt to forgive me for how I had treated him. He did so, and to this day I love him like my own flesh and blood.

One of my biggest regrets pushed me into reconciliation that became the foundation for a strong friendship. And who knows what the future holds? Perhaps Curt and I one day will work together again.

■ ■ ■

The journey from regret to regret-free is in large part one of going back through your past (even if that "past" is no further back than yesterday) and learning to soberly acknowledge those things you did that were unjust to others.

One of the most valuable tools you can take with you on such a discovery trip is being open to the truth that *we all tend to criticize in others what we are most insecure about in ourselves.* Whether or not we want them, our weaknesses sway our decisions and responses to the people and things around us.

When assessing what happened with a relationship that went south, carefully check to see if, without even realizing it, you were focusing on the little piece of wood in the other person's eye and ignoring the giant chunk of wood in your own. Chances are that in your past this has happened more often than you think.

It Does Take Two to Tango

So far we've been talking about how important it is to trace back and claim as your own responsibility whatever you did that later became a source of regret. And that certainly is something each and every person has to do (we'll return to this soon enough). The Lord doesn't reward people who don't admit their wrong-doing. He told Peter, "If I want [John] to remain alive until I return, what is that to you? As for you, follow me" (John 21:22). Jesus was saying what we all need to hear: Doing right by him is our personal responsibility, and we should never try to avoid or shirk it off onto someone else.

That said, what's also true is that it takes two to tango.

Now, just to be clear right up front, it doesn't take two to produce regret. Some of life's biggest regrets come from what we alone could have done but didn't, or what we alone wish we hadn't done but did. Sometimes it's just us, all by ourselves out on the sea, sailing our own boat, when we foolishly run it into a reef or clumsily ram it alongside a glacier. Sometimes when we crash and/or sink, there's just no one else around at whom to point the finger of blame.

The regrets I see causing the most pain, though—and the kind of regret that in my own life has caused the most pain—are from things having gone wrong between two people. Especially two who were, or were supposed to be, in partnership. When that sours, it leaves a terrible taste in everybody's mouth. An enemy can cause you plenty of pain, but *no one can hurt you like a friend who has become your enemy.* If it's you and a partner sailing that boat together, and one grabs the ship's wheel and purposefully runs it aground, *that* hurts.

What's important to remember, though, is that your shipmate *did* grab that wheel. It wasn't you or God or a distant relative possessing his body who steered the ship to wreckage. It was that person, and that person alone. Just like you have to take responsibility for whatever you did wrong in a relationship, so too does the other person have to take responsibility for what they did wrong in it.

It's absolutely essential that when assessing the origin and even nature of our regret, we take care not to take upon ourselves too much responsibility for what went wrong. It's just as easy—in some ways even easier, and (sadly) for a lot of us seems more natural—to take too much responsibility for a relationship that's turned out badly.

But we must remember that, in a way, claiming all or too much responsibility is just another form of ego gratification. It's a subtle form, to be sure, but it's ego all the same to assert that because of what *you* did, what *you* said, what *you* thought, the other person in the relationship suffered. That may in fact be the case; sometimes we do press our will upon another in such a way as to render them a victim. But most often the other person gave as well as they got. One of the biggest problems people have is that they like to act as if they're a victim, when in reality they're no more a victim than the guy at the carnival who willingly sits on the plank over the water so that paying customers can dunk him when their ball hits the bull's-eye.

When assessing the causes of your regret, remember, it takes two to tango. So tango on; but watch your step—and *only take responsibility when you miss the beat.*

Changing Your Perspective

One of the most dramatic biblical examples of personal regret occurred in connection with the Bible's most terrible event, the crucifixion of Jesus Christ:

> *When Judas, who had betrayed him, saw that Jesus was con-demned, he was seized with remorse and returned the thirty silver coins to the chief priests and the elders. "I have sinned," he said, "for I have betrayed innocent blood."*

"What is that to us?" they replied. "That's your respon-
sibility."

So Judas threw the money into the temple and left. Then he
went away and hanged himself. (Matthew 27:3–5 NIV)

Most people believe Judas went to hell for his sin against
the Lord. And he may have—but we won't know on this side
of heaven. Even though he did just about the most awful thing
anyone has ever done, we have no more place judging Judas than
we do anyone else. The job of ultimately judging *anyone* belongs
to God alone.

Nonetheless, from the passage above we can see clearly that
after his evil deed, Judas's attitude about what he'd done changed
a great deal. Soon thereafter he fell to his knees, desperately
despondent over his eager choice; he was "seized with remorse."
He was so distraught over his deliberate betrayal of Jesus that
the only way he could think to end his suffering was by ending
his own life.

What happened to Judas? How did he go from being a craven
opportunist to being consumed by burning remorse? How did he
go from wanting only money to being utterly desperate to possess
what money can't buy? What changed in the man?

What changed in Judas is the same thing that needs to change
in any of us seeking to come to terms with past regrets and learn
how to avoid creating new ones: *perspective.*

At first Judas's perspective was "What's best for me? What can
I do that most benefits me? How can I come out ahead?" He didn't
care who got hurt on his way to self-satisfaction; he just wanted
to know what he had to do to get what he wanted.

But that sure wasn't his perspective after he saw the results
of what he'd done. Suddenly his tragically limited, shamefully

selfish perspective became markedly broadened. With the force of a piano being dropped, Judas realized he hadn't been looking at a picture anywhere near big enough.

■ ■ ■

Put simply, perspective is everything. In my work at New Life, I'm made aware every day that the perspective people have on their problems is easily the most deciding factor on how effectively they'll be able to deal with them. In fact, I largely think of my mission as helping people to broaden their perspective. Take anyone with a problem. I want to show them the value of changing their perspective from one in which they're the center and star of the universe to one in which they realize that their world does, or should, revolve around the Son.

When assessing and evaluating a situation that led to your present regret, imagine yourself back in it—and then *try to see the whole of what happened not through your eyes but through God's.* Meditate on bringing the peace of the Holy Spirit to the situation that ultimately concluded so poorly. Picture yourself back with that other person in the relationship, and then lift your perspective so that it rises above the two of you here on earth. Strive, in other words, for a heavenly perspective from above.

> *Do not think of yourself more highly than you ought, but rather think of yourself with sober judgment, in accordance with the measure of faith God has given you.* (Romans 12:3 NIV)

Practice that—employ it when looking back on your regretful behaviors—and you'll be well on your way to feeling better about things you might have thought you could never feel comfortable with at all.

Two Wrongs Don't Make a Right

Every parent and teacher knows all too well the experience of having to deal with a child who thinks that the wrong thing they did is completely justified by the wrong thing first done to them. Billy steals Bobby's ball—so Bobby knocks over Billy's bike.

The question (and certainly as far as Bobby is concerned) is, are we ever justified in doing something wrong or destructive because someone else first did something wrong or destructive to us?

It's so easy for us to answer quickly with a resounding *no!* Straightaway we think of the Sermon on the Mount, where Jesus proclaims,

> *You have heard the law that says the punishment must match the injury: "An eye for an eye, and a tooth for a tooth." But I say, do not resist an evil person! If someone slaps you on the right cheek, offer the other cheek also.* (Matthew 5:38–39)

With that, we're sure that under no circumstances could we think it okay to respond to wrong by in turn doing wrong.

Turn the other cheek? Of course we would! We are, after all, dedicated followers of the Prince of Peace.

This is exactly how we feel about the matter—right up until the moment someone "slaps" us. For most of us, all bets are then *off.* Then, about the only cheek we're ready to turn is Mr. Slappy's—straight up to the sky as he spins to the ground from the clocking we just gave him.

■ ■ ■

My stepson does not fall into this particular category of "most of us." Last Saturday I watched him play basketball against a very tough and aggressive squad. He was on his game, scoring one-third of the points for the winning team.

Afterward, my wife, Misty, and I asked him how he had managed to handle with such equanimity the boy who kept shoving his hands in his face. Whenever that happened, he said, he thought of Jesus, and of how Jesus would want him to ignore it. He recalled the "turn the other cheek" passage. He's a pretty amazing boy. I wish we were all a little more like him when it comes to not reacting with vengeance.

But generally, for better or worse, we seem to have hardwired within us a strong sense that justice is served when someone has, at least in kind, done unto him whatever he did unto others. An eye for an eye and all that. It seems so simple and self-evident, hard to refute.

Hopefully, regrets about your past don't come from your having committed an actual crime or anything, but let's face it. When things get intense, most of us tend to react intensely. When voices get raised, we start yelling. When accusations start flying, we start launching them ourselves like Independence Day fireworks.

The ugly bottom line is that when things get bad, we very often get worse. And when we look back on such times, it's entirely too easy to let ourselves off the hook by claiming we weren't so much *acting* dishonorably as just *reacting* to something terrible.

All along in the back of our mind remains Jesus, directing us to repay evil with good—period.

When you assess the wrong you've done, be sure to hold yourself to Jesus' standard. Never exonerate yourself on the basis of what anyone said or did first. No matter how much you might tell yourself that what you did was justified, in your heart of hearts you know that in personal matters between two people, two wrongs never make a right.

If you're going to hold yourself fully accountable—which you must if you seek the full forgiveness that living regret-free demands—then all of your accounts must be on the table. No fair closing some books to scrutiny while opening others.

You can be forgiven for anything you did, but not if you don't bring everything you did before the Lord.

Here are a few pearls that help keep my other cheek turned:

Better a little with righteousness
  than much gain with injustice. (Proverbs 16:8 NIV)

When the storm has swept by, the wicked are gone,
  but the righteous stand firm forever. (10:25 NIV)

[Love] does not rejoice about injustice but rejoices whenever the truth wins out. (1 Corinthians 13:6)

CHAPTER 4

Stopping the Bleeding

Aaron couldn't breathe. He was starting to get dizzy. He was so hot he felt he was on fire. Everything was spinning out of control.

All around him alarm bells were telling him that if he didn't get it back under control, the spaceship he was piloting would start plummeting irretrievably downward, where it would burn up as it entered the earth's atmosphere. If that happened he, his two copilots, and everything his associates on the ground had worked so hard for would literally go up in flames.

And then, behind Aaron, smoke began pouring from the wall of the control cabin. He knew that in a matter of moments he wouldn't be able to see anything at all.

Do you know what Aaron made himself do, after he'd done the first thing he had to do, which is force himself not to panic? He made himself prioritize his needs—and *then* made himself forget about everything but his most important need. He determined right then that he needed to clear his head. Doing that, he knew, meant getting himself some oxygen.

So he forgot about the heat; he forgot about the alarms; he forgot about the smoke that was making everything disappear into a brown, churning fog. He merely reached for a mask, put it over his face, turned on a valve, and started breathing.

And that's when things for Aaron and his crew began to get better.

Ten minutes later he was emerging from the step module he'd been training in, to the applause of the testing crew, who had done everything possible to get Aaron to panic. And he hadn't. He'd held tight, remembered his training, and decisively acted to control the situation so it wouldn't control him.

That's the thing we need to do whenever one of our relationships threatens to go out of control. We have to act, and very often we have to act right away. And we always have to act right.

■ ■ ■

So far I've been focusing on how to relate to and deal with your regrets from the past. And of course that's very critical to do; after all, none of us has regrets about what we'll do sometime in the future.

Now, though, I'd like to move our attention from what happened in the past to what's happening right now. It's at least as important for us to live in the present so that we don't produce new regrets for our future.

The tricky thing about choices in the present that we end up regretting in the future is that we rarely do things *knowing* we're later going to wish we hadn't. When you're in the middle of a fight or enmeshed in a tough situation from which you can't see your way out, you don't spend a lot of time reflecting on everything going on around you. *Stepping back to meditate on the various momentary possibilities isn't common in tense situations.*

What you tend to do is act. Men and women react differently, but we all react. And when you feel threatened, angry, or embarrassed (or any such emotion), you usually react badly. You'd like to be stronger. You'd like to be wise enough to always do the helpful and productive thing. You'd like to say and do the things that will create *less* stress and tension.

But you don't. You get caught up in the moment, and you let the lower part of your nature take over a bit. You say the harsh or hurtful thing. You exploit the weakness of the one you're trying to beat. You see the possibility for advantage, and you take it.

You try to win. That's what people embroiled in conflict seek to do.

And sometimes you think—even without realizing you're thinking it—that if you can't win, you're going to take the other person down with you.

That attitude—that moment, right there, when you decide to go in for the emotional kill, when you fully unleash your inner mad dog, when you push down your better angel and bring in the worse—is where you always do and say what later, when everything is calm again, you regret.

This chapter is an attempt to show what we can do, even in the heat of an argument or at our lowest point, to avoid later feeling regret for what we did. It's possible to lead a regret-free life, and there's no better time to start than right now.

Emergency Triage

One of my favorite television shows has always been *M*A*S*H*. I have a friend named Tom who served in medical units in the Korean War, and he assures me that what I watch on *M*A*S*H* is very much like what he experienced. Except, judging from Tom's stories, the real thing was significantly less funny than the show.

"It was *M*A*S*H*, but without the jokes," he says. "And maybe other units did, but ours also didn't have any cross-dressers."

One of the things on *M*A*S*H* that's never funny, but always exciting and often inspiring, is when Hawkeye and the other doctors and nurses rush to greet the helicopters bringing in wounded soldiers from the battlefront.

"Triage!" goes out the call—then the jokes stop, the diversions are put away, and everyone immediately gets down to the serious business of making decisions that no one should ever have to make but that ER personnel make all too often.

What doctors have to decide during triage is who among those injured gets what treatment, and *in what order*. In this situation, you've got more injured people than medical personnel, so tough decisions have to be made in order to assure that the most good possible is done for the most patients possible. It's all about immediate assignations of available resources; whoever is in charge has the unenviable task of deciding who gets care right away . . . and who doesn't. And as vital as each of those choices is —and in large-scale emergencies like crashes or explosions, there can be many such needed decisions—it's not one personnel have the luxury of time to ponder. All they can do is assess, decide, execute, and move on.

A lot of times your emotional life can feel a bit like an emergency triage situation. You've said the harsh, angry thing. The other person has fired back a salvo that hit its mark.

Bullets are flying. Damage is being done. Alarms are going off.

People are getting hurt.

When you're in the middle of a situation, or when the situation has already happened and now the damage is left for you to deal with, what's to do? How to know where to start? What wound to treat first? What bleeding is most substantial? How do you even get the perspective in an "emergency" situation to know where you should begin?

How can you be calm when your defenses are up and crackling, when you're so emotionally invested in what's happened that you're maybe the last person who should be determining what steps should be taken to bring the most healing possible to the hurt parties? How can you play the role of doctor when you're also one of the wounded?

The answer is the answer to so many of our questions about how best to act in an emotionally tense situation: *Withdraw from the conflict.*

Withdraw. Step back. Take a second look.

Depersonalizing emotional volatility is an excellent way to help you examine and understand it. Imagine that whatever is happening to you is happening to someone else. I do this all the time; I imagine that I'm advising a friend going through the experience that's giving me trouble.

Purposefully taking yourself and your feelings out of a situation can give you keen insights. Have you ever noticed how wise you are when you're giving advice? You know why that is? Because detachment is to advice like syrup is to a pancake (makes it much better, and sweeter).

In a volatile emotional situation, whether it's you or the person you've hurt who needs the most help immediately, do the same thing in order to do the most good: Stop, take a breath, step back, and see what's happening not for what it looks like to you but for what it really is.

Imagine you're watching it on TV. And then, as quickly as you can, act to do the most healing possible.

The Wonder of Words

Do you know what, as a counselor, I consistently find to be the number one problem in marriages? You'd think it would be issues over money or sex, wouldn't you? It seems to me that I'm forever reading how these are the two subjects that cause couples the most trouble.

But that does not jibe with my experience. What I find by far to be the most divisive issue—the one that invariably *leads* to problems with sex and money—is that neither person is talking enough with the other.

Communication, communication, communication: the three most troubling aspects of most marriages I get involved with helping.

What's most interesting—and in a lot of ways simply hardest to believe—is the bottom-line reason for which most couples fail to adequately communicate. I call it the Carnac Syndrome.

Do you remember (if you're old enough to have seen it in the first place) the character Carnac the Magnificent that Johnny Carson used to play on *The Tonight Show*? The idea was that

Carnac had extraordinary clairvoyance; he was (or could be) a mind reader.

More often than not, if I'm dealing with a couple having problems with their marriage, the underlying reason is that either the husband or the wife thinks their partner is a mind reader.

They have Carnac Syndrome!

Here's how it works: The person with CS thinks the other should just know how they feel—should know (instinctively? telepathically? magically?) their deepest and most intimate feelings about whatever emotional dynamic is at hand. The weird thing is, the more important the issue is, the less likely the person with CS is able to make clear to their partner in any explicit way how they feel about it.

Once I parse out what's going on in a troubled marriage, the conclusion I almost inevitably reach is that the person with CS feels (whether or not they've yet realized it) that the closer an issue is to their heart, the more the other person should automatically be aware of it.

"This is something I'm terribly sensitive about!" they say. "You should know I feel _____ and _____! Don't you love me?"

Except, of course, they never actually say that. They don't say anything at all. They sit on the couch, brooding, because their partner didn't respond in the way they most wanted or needed.

If you want to avoid having regrets about a relationship, one of your first tasks is to make sure you're not suffering from Carnac Syndrome. Think about it. How many of your arguments are, when it comes right down to it, grounded in the way you think the person should already *know* how you feel? Especially when it comes to issues and dynamics you do indeed have a lot of feelings about?

I would go so far as to say that if you think you've never displayed CS symptoms, you're mistaken. In large part it's human nature to assume that someone to whom our heart is wedded does, or should, fully and utterly get us. Without analyzing the rationality of it, most of us just feel that this person should know our innermost thoughts, intuit our deepest feelings, handily anticipate our most profound needs.

And then they don't, and we resent them for it.

And that's one of the main places regrets start to take root.

Know this: No one can read the mind of another. It's not possible.

Your heart and mind belong to you and you alone. You're the only person with the key to that house. If you want to share it with someone (and you do, because that's what love's all about), you have to thoroughly communicate this. You have to invite the other person into your house.

You need to talk with your partner. Especially about things you really care about. If you're especially sensitive about your birthday or Christmas or sex or money, or about any of the sorts of things people tend to be especially intense about, talk about it.

Words can be the tonic that kills regrets before they have a chance to grow.

Always bear in mind that one never looks back on a relationship and wishes they had communicated less with the other person.

Be an Action Hero

Once upon a time, a fair maiden was kidnapped by a horrible ogre and forced to live alone in a hilltop castle tower surrounded by a deep moat, where purposefully underfed crocodiles lived.

Although she'd managed to fall into the ogre's clutches, the maiden was no idiot. Over the course of three years, working with a monk's patience, she managed to fill the hollow center of a feather with enough of her blood to write a note, make a little scrap of paper out of a patch of her gown, and train a bird to fly and fly and not stop until it landed on the shoulder of the first person it saw, as long as that person was no closer than one league from the castle.

One fine spring day, a knight on a mighty white steed heard something pecking on the side of his head armor. Lifting his face grate, he saw a bird sitting on his armored shoulder. On one of its legs was a note, secured there by (could it be?) a lock of golden hair woven into a delicate but strong braid.

"What's this?" said the knight. Meaning to lightly take hold of the bird, he squashed it instead; he'd forgotten to take off his iron gloves.

"Drat," said he. "Poor thing. But now, to the note!"

With increasing interest the knight read the maiden's message. He read about how she'd been kidnapped and was being held captive. The note even included the exact location of the castle in which she was being held. ("I taught myself astronomy," she'd written.)

"This is extraordinary!" declared the knight, rearing up his horse. "I shall this moment retire to my quarters and give this matter a great deal of consideration!"

And eventually the maiden died of old age in the tower.

■ ■ ■

So what went wrong? But of courseth: The knight did nothing. He needed to act, right? He was supposed to do something about that maiden in distress.

Alas, he failed. And we see what happened as a result.

Now, our good knight here seems uniquely dense, so it's not likely he's going to spend a lot of his life burdened with regret.

You, conversely, will, if ever you fail to take necessary action to secure the happiness of someone you are in relationship with.

If you are in a troubled relationship and want to avoid ever having regrets about the way you handled it, consider what you can actually do to help make things better. Words are good—words are great!—but oftentimes actions, as they say, speak even louder.

Give a massage. Buy and deliver a bouquet of flowers. Cook breakfast. Send brownies. Offer to change the car's oil. Do *something* to break the tit-for-tat pattern that in a problematic relationship so often takes on a toxic life all its own. Show the other person how determined you are to get things back on the right track.

Imagine if someone you're having difficulties with delivered chocolate to your office or brought a CD with all your favorite songs.

It could put things with him/her in a new perspective.

It could replace what would have probably become anxiety and regret with what is entirely more likely to become peace and resolution.

Keeping the Patient Alive

One of the key elements people fail to realize—a failure that often leads to having regrets—is that a relationship is *much* more than the sum of its parts. For most people, that's a radical concept.

Most of us are accustomed to things equaling the sum of their parts exactly. We know that 2 + 2 = 4; 4 + 4 = 8; 432 + 809 = some number I can't think of right now because with Attention Deficit Disorder I've already moved on to something else.

The point is, things usually equal the sum total of their parts.

But when it comes to that formulation, Christians have a slightly different take on it. There's at least one major instance where, instead of 1 + 1 + 1 = 3, it equals 1.

And to make it a little more confusing, that One equals everything.

You know what I'm talking about, right? The Father (one) + the Son (one) + the Spirit (one) = not three of anything but one almighty God.

$1 + 1 + 1 = 1$ = infinity googolazillion.

While being able to understand this broader application of numerical theory might make mathematics seem more confusing than we'd like (and when isn't it anyway, says I), it also gives the Christian a leg up in grasping an underlying truth.

It's this: In every two-person relationship of any consequence, there are three entities—the two people, and the relationship itself.

There's you, the other person, and the third *spirit*, if you will, that the two of you have created through your partnership.

And when a relationship goes bad—when it's become something that's going to lead to one or both parties having regrets—it's the third entity, the spirit of the relationship itself, that's hurting and in danger.

In this sense, the participants usually are doing well enough; most people, at any given moment of their lives—and especially when they're in a fight or having some kind of prolonged one-to-one struggle—are more or less convinced they're right and well and good and smart and strong. They're sharp; the *other* person is an idiot. That's how we tend to see things, right? *We're* okay; it's the other person who's broken.

Well, we're wrong about that—even if we are right about how wrong the other person is. It's not the other person who is broken or has become woefully dysfunctional. It's the *relationship* that is broken.

So much harm and pain could be avoided if one or both of the people involved would think not of themselves, and not really even of the other person, but of the relationship between them. That's what needs tending. That's what's hurt. That's what needs your love.

If a relationship you care about has gone sideways on you, try shifting your thoughts away from the other person and toward the non-corporeal but nonetheless utterly real entity that is the objective relationship the two of you have created.

Imagine that relationship is a real being that you care about, that you want to see healthy, vibrant, alive. If that being is hurting or even dying, you need to take whatever measures are necessary to keep the patient alive. You need to tend to it the same way you would anyone you cared about. You need to look at the relationship with that model in mind, as one that is suffering and maybe even expiring.

Focus on the relationship. You need to keep it alive. Give it CPR (which might be a dedicated day of alone time for the two of you to talk things out); give it a blood transfusion (which might be the two of you going to a counselor for perspective); put it in intensive care and monitor it day and night (which might be a vacation together). But do what you must to keep that patient alive.

Above all, don't be shy about asking the other person in the relationship's "trinity" to help you with keeping it alive. That you want to keep it vital is often all the other person needs to hear to inspire them to put their temporal differences with you aside, and to begin, hand in hand, healing the good thing the two of you have had together.

The Importance of Bedside Manner

One time I was in the hospital for a nasty infection that had settled in my lungs. As a result of my needing to be near the pulmonary specialists and equipment, I ended up staying three days and two nights in the emphysema ward. I was in a large room with three other patients, each of them suffering from advanced emphysema.

Halfway through my second day, one of the men began to cough vigorously. I was already used to hearing this (not that one can ever really get used to hearing an emphysema patient in a coughing jag), but it soon became apparent to the rest of us that this gentleman's cough was deeper and harsher than any we'd yet heard. Thirty or so seconds into his fit, it was clear my new friend was in trouble.

Before any of us could press the little buttons we all had near our beds, a strange thing happened. A priest passing outside our door heard the severity of the cough and came into our room.

The priest's appearance greatly excited the coughing man. He was advanced in years, already prone to excitement—he was the nervous sort, never comfortable, anxious about everything, as people get sometimes when (in my humble opinion) they're maybe a little bit closer to the reality of their passing than they're psychologically prepared to be.

At this point I'd been sharing a room with this man long enough to know that the last thing he needed to see, suddenly, in the middle of a coughing fit was a priest. The effect on him was terrible. His eyes got wide, and with a terrified expression he struggled to wave the priest away, all the while coughing with such violent force it lifted the whole top half of his body off his mattress.

The priest understood that his presence was hardly calmative, and he left to get a doctor.

I'll never forget the doctor who soon came striding into our room. He went to the bed, sat on it, and gently placed his hand on the old man's chest.

"Now, now," he said in warm, calm, soothing tone, "you'll be all right. You're fine. You're just fine." Almost immediately the old man's cough subsided and then stopped altogether. He lay back on his pillows and looked at the doctor as if looking at Christ himself.

In the next five minutes, listening to the way that good doctor spoke to his patient, I learned as much about the proper way to handle people in a personal crisis as I think I've ever learned at one time or from one person. The man was an inspiration. Calm, kind, respectful, caring, professional . . . his palliative effect was a marvel to behold. We *all* felt better, just from watching and hearing him interact with our roommate.

He didn't do anything special—beyond, that is, the most special thing anyone can ever do for another: *He showed that he cared.* Not as a matter of course. Not because he had to. And not because it was his job.

■　■　■

If you're in a relationship that is, shall we say, in the throes of a deep and painful coughing episode, try treating the other person as if you were a doctor and they were in need of care. Not condescendingly; not as if you have all the answers; not from the position of a superior to an inferior. Rather, as someone who, like our good doctor, really and truly cares. Behave like someone who sees the big picture—who knows what's right and what needs to be done; who is equipped and prepared to do whatever needs to be done in order to bring about full recovery.

Mostly, behave like someone who cares about the other person. For a moment, resolutely put aside your differences and sit beside your loved one. Reach out—figuratively and literally. Speak healing words in soothing, kind tones. Be sensitive to what they most need to hear to feel all right again. Help them understand that they're not alone—that, difficulties or not, you're still with them, will always care, and will be there for them no matter how rough things get.

Practicing a good bedside manner calls for you to be the kindest, wisest, most sensitive person you can be. There's never a better time to be that person than when you're in a relationship that you want to become a source of peace and productivity rather than anger and regret.

CHAPTER 5

When It's Not Getting Better

I don't like to admit it, but I have a competitive streak. It's not that I ever want to see another person do poorly. It's just that quite often (and, alas, always before I can stop myself) I find myself wishing the other guy would do just a little more poorly.

No example could be clearer than what I call the Reality Run.

The Reality Run began when I took my first jog with Misty. When she first asked if I was a jogger, I said, "Sure," because I did jog. Or, more precisely, I had jogged in the past. I knew *how* to jog, being the point. But I didn't see any reason to put up the entire history of my jogging life. So I just said, "Sure," and let it drop.

Except it didn't.

"Great!" Misty said. "Let's find a time today to put on the shoes and get in a good jog together."

"Sounds good!" I said. What the heck. I've always considered myself a bit of an athlete. I had running shorts. I had running shoes. I could hold my own.

Perhaps you see where this story is going.

Misty and I had run about a quarter mile when it occurred to me that she could have been training for the Olympics. She actually *was* training, it turned out, for a half marathon. Her pace was *fast*. I knew I could keep up—for a while. But I also knew that it was going to cost me.

About half a mile in, I felt my lungs aching.

After another quarter, I became aware of the distinct possibility I might suffer a stroke, or a coronary—or that I might simply faint, right there on the path.

A mile in, I was in such trouble that I finally asked if we could stop and take a break.

"Why not enjoy the scenery," I wheezed, "instead of just rushing through it?" I'm pretty sure Misty believed the only reason I wanted to stop was for scenery.

Not.

Suffice it to say, my desire to pretend everything was fine and my aversion to looking weak had made me run entirely too hard for entirely too long for my own good.

■ ■ ■

We sometimes do the same thing with our relationships. We believe they naturally can go the distance; we just keep driving forward with them. We fail to notice the toll our relationships are taking—the sheer wear and tear—until we're emotionally and even physically exhausted by what we've allowed them to do to us.

Sometimes what's happening to us in a relationship—and so necessarily to the person in it with us—is really hurting us. Sometimes continuing on the same path that's already proven difficult is bound, in the end, to do nothing but hobble us.

Sometimes no matter what we do, or how hard we try, things between us and the person simply aren't getting better.

Acknowledging that an important relationship has reached the critical point where, as is, it can no longer continue is one of the hardest things any of us ever has to do. If you're at that point in a relationship, please pay special attention to this chapter. I've been there and been through it. Let me help you make it through it too.

Trust me. You don't have to go on suffering.

The Importance of Honesty

You've no doubt heard the famous saying attributed to Abraham Lincoln: "You can fool some of the people all of the time, and all of the people some of the time, but you cannot fool all of the people all of the time."

To that I add, "You can't fool anyone with whom you're trying to heal a close relationship for any amount of time at all." You just can't. There are a lot of things you have to deal with when you're trying to heal a hurting relationship, but this is one of the biggest, and it's definitely one of the first to understand before going into the healing process.

The reason is that the other person knows you. In some ways, they know you better than you know yourself. They know how you react. They know which buttons are easy to push. They know what sorts of points you give in on and what sort you don't. They know how you like to think of yourself. They know how you like to think of them. They know what to expect of you.

Mostly what they know—and certainly what they think they know—is what's happened between you and them. Sure, you each might have different ideas about certain things that have transpired—but they do have a truth, with a giant T, that belongs to them alone, one that contains and informs for them the person they believe you to have been during the course of their experience with you. And they are as certain of the veracity of their interpretation as you are of the same.

This is right where the trouble usually begins, isn't it? Because so often what others believe is the truth of what happened doesn't strike you as the truth at all. Sometimes it even strikes you as pure, 100 percent cow doody. And then what should you do? How do you handle it when, in effect, your truth collides with theirs?

You make sure that every time you talk about what's happened, you're scrupulously, deeply honest with your version of it. There are lots of times in relationships where, for whatever reason, you're going to find yourself inclined to posture or challenge or duck responsibility. But none of those have any place in a relationship that you're wholeheartedly trying to ensure will produce no more regrets.

Christ says he is the Way, the Truth, and the Life. We want to be sure he is with us in everything we do, especially as we're trying to bring anything like Christ's healing to a relationship. Therefore, we must purposefully and tenaciously cling to the highest, broadest truth we can conceive of.

Being truthful to a degree worthy of God means so much more than simply not lying. It means we *take the time to discern what the truth is.* We have to know what happened, know who we are, know who we *were* when things went awry. We have to plumb the depths of our hearts and souls so that we can hear God telling us the truth of our situation—as opposed to the "truth" we would most like to be true (the one where we're always right and never wrong).

Only God knows who we really were at every point of our lives. And if we're going to be truthful about who we were in the course of a relationship—if we're going to align ourselves with God's truth, so that with its light we can find our way out of the darkness a relationship has become—then we need to pray. We need to ask God to put the truth of who we are and have been into our hearts. Then we can bring that truthful, honest heart to the other person.

Living a regret-free life means being honest about everything you did to help create your regrets and honest about how you felt when someone else was hurtful to you. That's a lot of honesty to be brought into your heart and mind. And it's not something you can bring to yourself. You must ask God to bring it to you.

Here are a few verses to bear in mind when you're doing that most important work. May they bless your life the way they have mine.

> *God has given both his promise and his oath. These two things are unchangeable because it is impossible for God to lie. Therefore, we who have fled to him for refuge can have great confidence as we hold to the hope that lies before us.* (Hebrews 6:18)

> *If you are faithful in little things, you will be faithful in large ones. But if you are dishonest in little things, you won't be honest with greater responsibilities.* (Luke 16:10)

> *Cling to your faith in Christ, and keep your conscience clear.* (1 Timothy 1:19a)

Doing All You Can

One time I was having coffee with a friend who told me his marriage was going through a very rough time.

"Oh, that's too bad," I said. "What's wrong?"

"She says I don't care enough for her. Or that I don't show her I care, or something. I don't know."

"Well, that's a little surprising, isn't it? Given you just bought her that ring, and all." Not two weeks before, we'd gone shopping for an anniversary gift, and he'd purchased his wife a lovely diamond ring.

"I know!" he said. "That was a great ring, right?"

"It sure was," I said. Then—knowing a thing or two about my friend—I asked, "Wait. How did you give her the ring?"

"What do you mean?"

"I mean, how did you give her the ring? Wrap it? Surprise her with it in some way? Anything like that? How did you *give* the ring to her?"

"I don't *know*," he said. "I gave it to her. That's the point."

"Well, *how'd* you give it to her?"

"I put it on the bed when we got home from shopping."

"Excuse me?"

"Why are you looking at me like that? I put it on the bed. I knew she'd find it when she got home from work. She did. She got the ring."

"You just put it on the bed for her? Did you wrap it or anything?"

"No, the box was nice enough."

"Are you kidding me? Did you even take it out of the bag?"

"Look—she wanted a ring. I knew it was going to be a big deal if I didn't get her a ring. So I did. I went shopping; we found a nice ring; I brought it home and gave it to her."

"No, you put a bag on the bed that had a ring in it. You practically treated it like garbage. Not exactly the Prince Charming method of giving a ring to the love of your life, you troglodyte." (This might be a good time to mention that he and I have been friends for a very long time.)

■ ■ ■

My friend was definitely not doing all he could in his relationship with his wife. When they finally got themselves into counseling, he came to have some very real regrets about this. But the important thing is that he understood how vital it was to do everything he could to make his marriage everything it could be. He learned it before it was too late—before he had a bunch of regrets *and* an empty bed at night.

Those two things are *not* fun to have together. Believe me, I know.

Paul says, "Let's not get tired of doing what is good. At just the right time we will reap a harvest of blessing if we don't give up" (Galatians 6:9). If that isn't the very formula for living a regret-free life, I've never read one. It isn't the easiest thing in the world to do, but you know the biggest rule of all for doing it: *Try your best.* Give it everything you have.

The catch is, you, and only you, know when you have, in fact, given everything to a relationship. This brings us back to the importance of honesty. Be honest with yourself about whether you are, every single day, in every single way, doing every single thing you can do in order to make any relationship you say you care about be as good as it can be.

If not, you've got to kick into a different gear. Make that additional gesture. Go that extra mile. Do that unexpected thing. Show that person you love them; don't just expect them to somehow know it.

"Never get tired of doing good" (2 Thessalonians 3:13b).

Knowing When Your Hand's Been Forced

Counselors, pastors, psychiatrists, and many others whose work entails helping people achieve peace and harmony have recently made a startling discovery. At first researchers were unconvinced by the data; the findings were too astounding to be accurate. So back to the drawing board and laboratory they went.

Eventually, though, they had no choice but to face it. Every test showed the same extraordinary results.

Unavoidable conclusion: Every relationship has two people in it.

Shocking, huh? Further reflection might reveal that you, too, have sensed the truth of this amazing phenomenon. You've probably noticed that no matter what you do, how hard you try, or what amazing plans you have for the overall good of any relationship, there's always the other person, waiting to make absolute hash out of the delicious, high-quality victuals you've placed on the table before them.

It's just the darnedest thing, isn't it? You've got all the answers, which means everything between you and the other person should be absolutely perfect. But it isn't.

And why? Because they keep asking all the wrong questions!

Ah, what a perfect life we'd all have, if only everyone we're in relationship with would realize the wisdom of our ways.

But they won't—and that's probably the number one reason more and more people prefer to cultivate cyber-relationships. In a "virtual" relationship, you're virtually the only one whose feelings and opinions you really have to consider. If you don't like what the other person has said, all you have to do is switch screens, or log out and then pretend to be somebody else. In cyberspace, you don't have to boldly (or not) go anywhere you don't want to go.

Not true in actual time and space, though, is it?

■ ■ ■

We've been having some fun with it, but of course there's nothing funny at all if you ever come to a point in an important relationship where you're stuck facing the fact that you're the only one who really cares if it gets saved or not.

That point usually comes when you discover the other person has left you no way of resolution. They've backed you into a corner, cut off further avenues of exploration, denied any and all potential.

In one way or another—usually, very explicitly—they've told you that it's over.

We all hate it when that happens. Even when it happens with a relationship you might have wanted to end, it still hurts—or at the very least irks—to be essentially told you have to give up on it. And it hurts all the more to find out that a relationship for which you were still nurturing hope is utterly hopeless. It's awful to learn that the time of a relationship you thought still had mileage has been spent; that you have arrived, but that, as it turns out, you've both been going to different places.

Sometimes that happens. Sometimes the other person does force your hand, does force you to realize their version of what's happened is going to win out; they're going to close the door to any more dialogue.

Where once you had two, now there is one. And that one is you.

That's a very tough time indeed. But it's one you can survive.

I was once talking at a conference with a woman who for eight years had been engaged to a man with a sexual addiction. I asked her why she'd held on to the relationship as long as she had, when he'd made no movement toward recovery or getting help. Her answer: She thought he needed more love, and that once she'd given it, he would change.

She asked for my advice, and I told her I thought she should end her engagement and move on.

If she were married to this man, I would have advised differently. I would have recommended that she hold off any movement toward ending the marriage, for then the way to avoid regret would have been to do whatever she could to help heal her husband and save her marriage. I would have encouraged her to get support rather than an attorney.

Not all important relationships, however, will transform for the better; sometimes one of the people is simply not willing to do the work. But before you give up, be sure that you do put forth the effort to make that relationship all that it could be. If it does end, and you can't fix it, then you'll want to know, for the rest of your life, that you did everything you could to make it right. If you don't do that, you'll always regret it.

Breaking Up Is Hard to Do

Relational regrets can come from anywhere along the time line. But the place where regrets are most likely to originate is at the end. Though you wish you didn't, the fact is you probably know more than you'd like about how that goes. We all do; we've all been through it. You do your best to maintain your dignity, but as a relationship falls apart in your very hands—and despite whatever effort you might put forth—you sometimes just wind up "losing it."

And by "it," I mean, of course, one of the two or three most precious things you own: your dignity.

The reason we end up feeling the loss of our dignity with the special depth of pain is that no one ever *takes* our dignity. No one ever steals or misplaces our dignity; no one ever stashes our dignity away in a drawer somewhere and then later can't remember where they put it. There's only one way anything as near and dear as our dignity ever gets lost, and that's if we lose it ourselves.

To lose your dignity means to betray yourself. And you never feel any regret as deeply as that of having betrayed your own self. You know how they say that the closer a person is, the more hurt they can cause? No one's closer to you than you—and so no one can hurt you more.

When you know a relationship is coming to a close—especially if it's very special to you, one you've put your heart and soul into—one of the most important things you can do is stop, collect yourself, and make sure that, before proceeding any further into dark, cold waters, you wrap up and protect your dignity.

Before you go into battle, you wouldn't lose track of your armor, would you? You wouldn't forget to feed your horse or leave your weaponry disconnected and lying all about. Those are the very things you'd need in order to come out of impending trial as strong as you can. If you're going to win an important struggle, you don't leave behind the very elements most likely to help you achieve the desired result.

And there's no such thing as being victorious and losing your dignity. Lose your dignity, lose. Keep your dignity, win. It's that simple.

Make no mistake. When you're in a relationship that's breaking up—one that can't be rescued, one in which the other person isn't going to accept anything but a complete break from you—you are in a war. It's an emotional war, but it's no less brutal for that. And you want to come out knowing you didn't say or do anything for which you are bound to have regrets.

That's a tall order, but it's one you can fulfill. To do so—to make sure that you, for one, leave any finally broken relationship behind without any regrets following you in its wake—"all" you have to do is make sure that throughout the course of the split, you never, ever sacrifice or compromise your dignity.

How? The same way you do anything that's critical, huge, and more than you could possibly do yourself. You call upon the Lord.

Put on every piece of God's armor so you will be able to resist the enemy in the time of evil. Then after the battle you will still be standing firm. Stand your ground, putting on the belt of truth and the body armor of God's righteousness. For shoes, put on the peace that comes from the Good News so that you will be fully prepared. In addition to all of these, hold up the shield of faith to stop the fiery arrows of the devil. Put on salvation as your hel- met, and take the sword of the Spirit, which is the word of God. (Ephesians 6:13–17)

No relationship is worth the dignity and honor that comes from knowing you are with God. Hand in hand with Jesus, always walk proud.

Biting the Bullet

A friend of mine, whom I'll call Lucinda, was not doing a very good job of releasing from her life a man I'll call Ken. Lucinda and Ken had been dating for about two years. Then Ken wanted to move on.

Lucinda, however, had other plans. She felt that, contrary to what Ken had told her, the relationship *wasn't* over. She was con- vinced that if she just said, did, or even thought the right thing, Ken would realize how foolish it was to think he could live the rest of his life without the only woman in the world God wanted for him.

"But, Lucinda," I said one afternoon over coffee, "you've got to let go. You can't force a man to be in a relationship with you. You can't trick him into wanting to continue to care for you. You can't trap him. You know the saying about the proof of your love being your ability to let a person go? I think Ken wants to be let go, Lucinda. If you really love him as you say, you will *let* him go, because you want him to be happy. If he knows he would be happiest without you, then in honor of him you must honor that. You can see that, can't you?"

Alas, she was too wrapped up in Ken to hear anything else.

It was disheartening to see Lucinda going further and further down in her efforts to reclaim for herself the relationship with Ken she'd once enjoyed. (To be honest, I thought a big part of her problem with Ken—who, for the record, I always thought a bit of a jerk—is that she never really *had* enjoyed the relationship. He was mean to Lucinda, a godly woman who deserved a man who put her feelings and needs first.) She basically became obsessed. She was always checking her phones to see if Ken had called; she would send him loads of e-mail and was always calling him fairly late at night, knowing he'd be home.

Then she began driving to his job and parking near his car when he'd be getting off work, and I began to see real problems.

If you're in a relationship where it's time for you to bite the bullet and finally let go, I'll give you the same advice I finally gave to Lucinda (which, I'm happy to report, she took).

Let it go. Recognize when it's over and let it die the natural death it should. If you keep the relationship raggedy—if you cling to what's fallen apart, if you continue to engage someone trying to disengage, if you keep chasing something that keeps running away from you—you're only going to make things grow worse until finally, inevitably, you could very well have on your hands something approaching a tragedy.

You can't force a person to have feelings, convictions, and loyalties. It's like trying to get water to run any way but downhill; it's just not going to happen. If you try to force someone, they're going to resent you with every fiber in their being. It's not probable that that will happen; it's not likely. It's 100 percent *guaranteed.* It can't happen any other way. People know what they want and what they need. If someone you think you want and need has decided they don't want and need you, then the sooner you realize you *must* let that relationship go, the better.

Because, in truth, you don't need him or her. You may think you do, but that's a temporary condition. It will pass. You need to let it pass so that you can move on and find someone who does connect with you in a way that's healthy, productive, and fulfilling in the loving way God intends for all of his children.

If you are already married, it is a bit different than just letting the person go. Often, married couples go from doing nothing to considering divorce. Rather than go from one extreme to another, do some things that might bring healing. After all, when a person repeatedly hurts us, our reaction often "trains" the person to do it. Don't go from training, enabling, and allowing to leaving. If, however, the other person has already divorced you, you have to decide to pick up your life and let go of what was or what might have been.

Six Qualities of a Happy, Regret-Free Relationship

The Christian mystic Leo Tolstoy opened one of his greatest novels, *Anna Karenina*, with one of the most quoted lines in literature: "Happy families are all alike; every unhappy family is unhappy in its own way."

That, right there, should give you every last reason you'd ever need to read *Anna Karenina*. But that's a conversation for another day. For now, let's think a little about the meaning of that thought.

Is it true? *Are* all happy families alike?

And if it's true (Tolstoy was, after all, one of the most astute students of human nature who ever lived—so, safe to guess that it is), then does that mean every healthy relationship of any kind is the same as any other of that same kind? Does it mean that a healthy relationship between any particular father and son is substantially the same as any other between a father and his son?

Are the dynamics inherent in a healthy relationship between a husband and wife essentially equal to the same sort experienced between any other happily married couple?

Is love really the same, wherever it manifests?

I think it is. I think that we, as individual people, can make a mess of our lives and our relationships—can give ourselves and others more regrets than we or they will ever know what to do with—in ways so unique to us personally that no one can possibly imitate or duplicate. I can manipulate my child, or undermine my wife's confidence, in a way that is inimitable. No one can insult me like my own father can; no one can hurt me like my own mother. No one can upset a protégé like his mentor. No one can get under one's skin like her sibling. No one can disappoint a parent like his or her child.

And on and on and on.

We dysfunction as we live—as separate, distinct individuals. That's the gist of much of the bad news that sooner or later we all face in life.

And yet we can rejoice! For we love as God loves us; filled with the love of the Lord, we love others in the only way love ever acts.

> *Love is patient and kind. Love is not jealous or boastful or proud or rude. It does not demand its own way. It is not irritable, and it keeps no record of being wronged. It does not rejoice about injustice but rejoices whenever the truth wins out. Love never gives up, never loses faith, is always hopeful, and endures through every circumstance.* (1 Corinthians 13:4–7)

That is true for every kind of love, between every kind of person.

Let's take a look now at universal signs of a healthy relationship.

Affection

There was a time in my life when I thought my destiny was to be a major star of Broadway musical theater. I imagined myself bright in the footlights, belting out the show tunes that make women break down and cry, as men stalwartly pretend they're not about to do the same. Even though I was later forced to realize my singing voice was making people cry for reasons I never intended, I've remained a great fan of live theater.

I'm particularly fond of amateur theater. There's just something I find touching about people coming together in their community to mount a play.

After one such play I experienced a display of affection that to this day moves me to remember. I was backstage after a community theater matinee performance that featured a dear friend of mine. I was sitting off in a corner, watching everyone involved or connected with the play interact together in that happy, lively, pumped-up fashion folks do after the curtain has dropped and they've regrouped again. Then, into the room came the family of a young man who'd had a relatively small but nonetheless important role. They were a shy group—until they spotted the object of their affection.

A young girl—the boy's sister, I supposed—squealed, held out her arms, and ran to him. The young actor's mother beamed and followed her daughter. The father looked a little awkward as he made his way across, but once near he smiled broadly and embraced his son in a hug that threatened to cut off the boy's oxygen.

A teen near to the actor's age—a brother or cousin, I supposed—shyly offered his hand to the actor, and then, too excited for such a modest display of affection, also hugged his compadre. A little girl who'd come in with the family clung to the young man's leg. Another little girl, maybe ten years old, bounced on her toes and rapidly clapped her hands together in anticipation of the moment that she too would be able to show how much she loved the star of the day.

I was fascinated and deeply touched by this show of affection. It was so spontaneous, so real, so deeply felt. And it was such an intimate and personal moment for them that before too long politeness compelled me to look away. And that's when I saw that there was nothing but such affection on display all over that spacious room. Everywhere I looked I saw people hugging, shaking hands, patting one another on the back, laughing, smiling, encouraging, supporting.

Loving.

In one way or another, it was all love. Whether paternal, fraternal, romantic, or friendly, it was, in essence, the same. What everyone in that room was showing to someone else was *love,* pure and simple.

Affection is love shown. You can always tell when one person loves another; they can't help but in one way or another show it through their body language, gestures, words. And consistently too; feelings of affection are obvious to anyone who takes a moment to see it. A love never manifested—never displayed, never acted upon, never brought forth from the private heart to the public sphere—is no love at all. It is love's very nature to express itself; displays of affection are what love looks like. And that's why, in every relationship based on love, you see them everywhere.

Respect

One of the most charming things in the world is to be around two people who respect each other. It shows in the gleam in their eyes when they look at one another, the readiness with which they laugh at each other's jokes, the supportive tones in which they speak. There's no mistaking respect for any other personal quality, because no other quality looks and acts the same way.

When I think of people for whom I have particular respect, my mind first goes to the women in my life. I am so fortunate to have women around me that I truly respect. I have a mother who is strong, faithful, and persevering. I respect my daughter, Madeline, a young woman of strong character and astute sensibilities.

And finally I respect my wife. Misty is a woman of courage who does whatever it takes to overcome her fears. She is willing to face her demons in counseling and recovery. She is a great friend and a wonderful romantic. And what a mother she is! She raises our children with the perfect combination of love, connection, boundaries, and grace.

The interesting thing about *respect*—the important thing we must not forget if we want to be sure our relationships are infused with all of it they should be—is that *it doesn't really work if it's not there 100 percent*. People can sense when you don't respect them all the way. And for most people, knowing you don't respect them 100 percent feels the same as if you didn't respect them at all.

People want (and, to a very real extent, need) full respect. Half respect is like a pair of pants with one short leg—it just doesn't feel right.

The problem, of course, is that not everybody feels or is worthy of your true respect. And that's not usually a problem—unless the person you aren't inclined to respect much happens to be someone with whom you're supposed to be in a caring relationship. Then your lack of respect can be a whole load of trouble.

What do you do in a case like that? How do you respect someone you're not inclined to?

Well, the first thing you have to do is make sure that before you even get involved with the whole dynamic of bestowing your respect upon another, you've first bestowed it upon yourself. "Respect yourself" is a pretty standard saying, but like "Look both ways before you cross the street," this advice you should never fail to take. Many clichés become clichés because they make so much sense that people keep repeating them all the time. Regardless, that doesn't make truth any less true. And no cliché says more in fewer words than "Respect yourself."

Respect is crucial to relational health. And again, you can't respect anyone else if you don't first respect yourself. In a way, this feels counterintuitive, but anything contrary is an illusion.

You can admire someone if you don't respect yourself. You can envy them. You can crave their attention. You can have all kinds of emotions toward them. But you can't ever truly respect them.

The reason? The degree to which you don't respect yourself is the degree to which you will be unable to transmit to anyone else something as pure and steady as respect. It's that painful, that simple, and that true. A person who doesn't respect herself trying to feel and show respect for another is like a person strapping heavy weights onto her arms and legs, jumping into a pool, and trying to swim. She's merely going to sink.

So how do you learn to respect yourself? You *give yourself credit* for everything you are and have done that's valuable and worthy of respect, you *forgive yourself* for your failures, and you *respect the potential* of what you could become.

In other words, you *see yourself the way God sees you*. God created you and loves you; and that means he's proud of everything good you've ever done. He sent his one and only Son to die for your sins; that means he forgives you for everything wrong you've ever done. And Jesus has promised us everlasting life; that means he's excited about all the good he knows is in your future.

Let God love you. Respect yourself for being deemed worthy of that love, and then make sure to extend to others—and especially to anyone you care about—the same respect God has given you. Respect anyone you're in relationship with for who they are and for who, God knows, they might yet become.

And then forgive them, as God has forgiven you.

Shared Values

A good friend of mine was kind enough to share with us this story:

> When I was a new college student, I had an experience that I always recall whenever I think of how great it is for people in a relationship to share common values.
>
> I had been invited to go with a few other students to the home of a married couple. The husband of the couple taught history at the college I was attending. His wife was also an educator. At the time the couple seemed quite old; looking back, I see the husband and wife were then about the same age that I am now—which is to say, amazingly young, yet fully in the prime of their life.
>
> I didn't know the couple at all before I met them that afternoon. I don't even remember exactly why I had been invited to their house; I believe it was part of the college's "Meet the Faculty" effort, part of the freshman orientation program. All

I knew is that I was supposed to go, and that we'd be served food. When you're nineteen, knowing you'll get food is all the reason you need to show up anywhere.

The couple was from Poland, and they were just about the nicest people you'd ever want to meet. They cooked and served us a splendid meal, and afterward invited us into their living room, where the seven or eight of us sipped sweet tea and talked about the college, what we expected from it, and so on. It was a very pleasant couple of hours.

As we were all standing to leave—getting our coats and gloves and so on—the husband quietly took me aside and asked if I'd mind staying behind the others. I said of course I wouldn't—and before too long my fellow students were all gone from the place, and then it was just the couple and I.

"Won't you have a seat?" said the wife, indicating the couch from which I'd so recently risen. "Would you like more cookies?" I allowed as how I would. While she disappeared into the kitchen, and her husband was out of the room for a moment, I sat, wondering what it was this sweet and interesting couple wanted to talk to me about in private.

Soon they returned to the room, and what they shared with me was that they had sensed that I, unlike the other students who'd just left, wasn't really sure about what field I wanted to major in—that, basically, I still didn't know what I wanted to be when I grew up. They were right; I didn't. What the husband and wife wanted to communicate to me was that this was all right; it was very important that I not feel rushed to declare a major but instead remain open to the wonders and allurements of all fields of discipline.

"What is important is education itself," said the man. "To develop one's mind is the highest and most rewarding endeavor there is."

"Never think of education as a means," said the wife. "It's an end in itself. A well-developed, informed mind is the greatest asset one can have in this life."

We spoke together for the next half hour or so, and in that time I came to see how utterly and completely this couple was devoted to education. He was a professor at my college (and, I learned soon enough, a wildly popular one at that); she taught at a local junior college, as well as wrote and edited college-level liberal arts textbooks. And being with this enthusiastic, articulate, good-natured couple was like being in the middle of an ongoing love-fest for education. They believed in education, they knew it was fantastic, they cared that as many young people as they could reach learned to love education as much as they did.

They had a shared value at the core of their relationship. It was something bigger than they; something with universal import; something they could never outgrow.

A love of education wasn't tangential to this relationship; it was core. Their relationship largely was built upon it. I find it inspiring to hear how this couple had allowed something good they both believed in to become their focus and purpose—how they used that shared value to, in a sense, put the lives of countless others before themselves.

If you want to establish a good and healthy relationship with someone, find out what values you share and then build upon those. Maybe it's the job you both work at. Maybe it's common family members. Maybe (hopefully!) it's God. But whatever it is, find it, claim it—and then start to build your relationship upon it.

Honesty

I suppose if there was one quality I would wish defined every relationship in the world, it would be honesty. If two people are honest with each other, there is no kind of woe they can't survive. Hard times and difficult passages come to everybody, but it's those who are honest with themselves and their loved ones who always weather them best.

Dishonesty is poison in a relationship. That's because lies never really go away. If you lie, you always know you lied—and that becomes a reality that does nothing but corrode everything it touches. Since what you do with a lie is hide it in your heart, it corrodes everything your heart touches—which means it corrodes virtually everything in your life. Who ever goes anywhere, ever does anything, or ever thinks or feels anything at all without their heart being involved?

Putting a lie in your heart (which, again, is the only place you can hide a lie) is like putting a pile of cow manure right in the middle of your living room. It gradually ruins the place.

Have you ever been in a relationship in which you can tell the other person isn't being completely honest with you? There's hardly anything else you can discover about your spouse, friend, child, or parent that hurts more than that they're lying to you. Learning you're being lied to can feel like a two-by-four right across the back of your head. It hurts like heck and makes you a little nauseated.

One of the reasons being lied to hurts so much is that once you've discovered one thing, you have no idea how many other things are lies. A saying that should be but isn't as well known as "Respect yourself" is "Liars lie." Lying is what liars *do*. Lying once about something small makes it easier to lie later about something a little larger—and then a little larger, and then a little larger still. Next thing you know, you can't be honest if someone asks you what time it is. That's what happens to people who allow themselves to take on the habit of lying. After a while they've told so many lies to so many people over so much time that, without even realizing it, they've come to believe what liars always believe, which is that the truth is relative.

Unfortunately, we all know people who, when push comes to shove, believe this. Such people tend not to lie in big, overt ways—by telling you, for instance, that they're directly related to King Henry VIII or that it was their father and not Henry Ford who really invented the steam-combustible automobile engine. Instead, they fuzzy the truth all the time; they tweak it here and there to serve their purposes; they consider the truth a malleable thing they can shape and shift into whatever they need or prefer it to be.

And such people invariably leave you unable to believe anything they say, even though 99 percent of it might be true.

Liars lie. If someone would lie to you about one thing, they could lie to you about anything at all.

Be honest in everything you do, and insist on honesty from anyone with whom you share a relationship. This is the one thing that can't be compromised or worked around; if the other person can't or won't be utterly honest with you—even if it's just to tell you how much trouble they have being really honest with you or themselves—then understand how unlikely it is that you'll have a relationship with them that's really of any consequence. Honesty is to a relationship what mortar is to a brick house; without it, you simply can't build.

With it? The sky's the limit.

Trust

People are fond of telling others how important trust is to a relationship. But have you ever thought about what that really means? What *is* trust, anyway? Is it knowing that if you give someone $10,000 in cash and ask them to take it to the bank, they won't hop on a bus and leave town with your money? Is it knowing that if another person tells you that one time they swam across the English Channel in a wedding gown, then, by golly, you can be sure that it actually happened? Is that what trust is? Does trusting someone mean you can always count on them to do the right thing, act the right way, be at all times the person you would most prefer them to be?

The answer is yes. Trust is all those things. But it's more. Or rather, it's less—it's even simpler than all of those things.

You know what I think trust is? I think it's *an assurance of love.* The people I trust in my life are the people that I know love me. That's it. That's how I know someone is as trustworthy as I need him or her to be: They love me.

Now, that said, it's important to note that for someone to have my absolute and unswerving trust I have to know that they *really* love me. They can't just like me. They can't just be pretty fond of me. They can't just think I look good in a particular suit or greatly enjoy the way I spoke at the conference they attended. No, they have to love me. Deeply. Sincerely. Honestly. Truly.

Love me; deserve my trust. That's my motto. Someone who really loves someone else would no sooner hurt that person than they would purposefully shoot off their own foot. Trust, in the end, is a very personal thing; we trust the people in our lives whom we are sure wouldn't hurt us on purpose. And we only feel that way about people we love. It's why most people trust their mothers.

Their very instinct is that of all the people in the world least likely to hurt them, their mother is number one.

Now, if you're in a relationship with someone you don't entirely trust, consider: That means you sense that person doesn't really love you. Different way of looking at that problem, isn't it? Looking at it thus means that not trusting the other person isn't the problem; it's a *symptom* of the problem. You don't think he loves you. You feel like he doesn't love you, and that means you feel you can't trust him. The reason you feel this way is you know that at some point a person who doesn't love you *will* separate your interests from his. And you know whose interests he will protect and support: his.

And you know what that means to you: You'll be out in the cold.

There are two kinds of people I don't implicitly trust: strangers, and people whom I don't feel confident love me unconditionally. That doesn't leave a whole lot of names on the list of people I trust implicitly. But the ones who are on it have earned their place, and it's carved there in gold. These are the people who are dearest to me.

If you're in a relationship with someone whom you should trust but don't, think about why it is you perceive that person doesn't love you. Have you done something to make it so they can't? Has there been some misunderstanding that has reasonably led them not to love? Talk with them about it. Tell them you want to be close to them—that you want to share a real and solid love, so that your relationship can be everything that, at heart, you both want it to be.

Grow love, and trust will follow.

Freedom to Be

"Freedom to be *what*?" you may be asking. "Santa Claus? A traveling apron salesman? A circus freak? What do you mean, 'freedom to be,' Steve?"

Hey, what's wrong? Don't you trust me? How can you not? Don't you know how lovable I am? (Note: This will not be funny unless you've read the previous section on trust. I trust you will go do that now.)

As a matter of fact, I do mean free to be Santa Claus—and/or, for that matter, a circus freak. (You are also, I should say, entirely free, as far as I am concerned, to go off and become a traveling apron salesman. And if you do pursue that singular career, may I just say, "Good luck.")

One of the qualities that's always present in a healthy relationship is that each person in it is free to be whoever they care to be.

My wife knows most of the plot lines and some of the dialogue from *Seinfeld* and *Friends*. It seems every situation in life has been covered by at least one of those two shows. One episode of *Friends* showed very well the importance of allowing and encouraging someone with whom you're in relationship to be and become what they like. The plot had to do with Rachel being profoundly uncomfortable with the way Phoebe *ran*.

One day Rachel, a runner, asks Phoebe (whose apartment she had just moved into; even better, for the point I'm making here, is that Rachel and Phoebe's friendship had assumed this new intimacy) if she'd like to come on a run with her.

"It'll be fun," says Rachel. "We'll run in the park. It'll be our first roommate bonding thing!" Phoebe, happy to come along, joins Rachel on her run through New York's lovely Central Park.

And that's when Rachel discovers that when Phoebe runs, she throws her arms and kicks her legs around in a way that Rachel finds positively mortifying.

Later, when she's with a few of her other friends, Rachel tells them that because of Phoebe's spastic running style ("When she runs, she looks like a cross between Kermit the Frog and the Six Million Dollar Man"), she never again wants to be seen running with her roommate. Her friends wisely tell her to be honest with Phoebe. Rachel assures them that she will—but then, when Phoebe asks her about the two of them running together again sometime, Rachel lies and says she's hurt her foot and can't go running again, "probably forever."

Later, of course, Phoebe catches Rachel running and confronts her. Rachel then tells the truth about why she doesn't want to go with her anymore. Phoebe explains that she knows what a goof she looks like when running but that she still prefers to run that way.

"I run like I did when I was a kid," she explains, "because that's the only way it's fun."

Later, Rachel sees the mistake of putting her need to conform over and above her friend's need to be herself. (And, in fact, Rachel tries her way of running and finds it wildly liberating—until she runs smack into a policeman's horse.)

But there's the whole dynamic, in a nutshell: If Rachel is going to be in a healthy relationship with Phoebe—if she's going to really and truly love Phoebe—then she is going to have to let Phoebe be Phoebe. That's one of the big rules of being in a loving, trusting relationship. *You let them be them, and they let you be you.*

If you're in a relationship where you don't feel free to be and explore every possible dimension of yourself, stop and question why. Is it because you aren't comfortable fully exploring yourself, or is it because you feel the other person wouldn't be comfortable with you being yourself? If it's the former, trust that God will always love and support you—especially if you're seeking to make more of yourself or to more creatively or fully express yourself. If the reason you hesitate to be free expressing and being yourself is that you sense doing so would in some way upset the person with whom you're in relationship, talk to that person about it. Share with them what you *want* to be and do.

Chances are you'll be surprised by how open the other person is to your being as open with them about yourself as you'd like to be. Sharing your uniqueness is one of the best ways to show that person how much you care about and trust them. It's a very tangible way of putting your love for them into action.

Sometimes letting go and trusting God means letting go and trusting the person with whom it's clear God wants you to grow. Don't be afraid to be you. If that hurts your relationship, it has bigger problems than that you, say, run funny, or want to be a traveling apron salesman.

And in the same spirit, be sure to always invite your partner to be exactly who they are and who they want to be.

CHAPTER 7

Dropping
Your Baggage

Whenever you're in a room with another person, you're not really alone with that person at all. In that room are at least fourteen people—and that's if neither you nor the other person have any siblings. At an absolute bare minimum in that room are you, your parents, your parents' parents—and also the other person, their parents, and their parents' parents.

Quite a little crowd! Throw in a brother and sister here and there, and you've got enough for a whole hockey team.

Everywhere you go, you bring with you not only your physical heritage but also your emotional heritage. Your attitudes, expectations, insecurities, fears, convictions, assumptions, coping mechanisms . . . it all comes to you from your parents—who, in turn, inherited it (and more) from their parents.

Saying that you are the sum result of the inherited physicality and psychology of your ancestors is not the same thing as saying you have no choice about who you are. Each of us ultimately is in control of who we are and who we become. We're not simply clones of our parents.

But to deny the power of your inherited legacy from generations past, woven deep into the very fabric of not just how you look but also how you think and feel, is to deny the reality of one of the most powerful determining forces at work in your life. You do pick up your parents' attitudes. You incorporate their worldviews into your own. You learn to relate to members of the opposite sex in the way they did. You bond in the way they bonded. In one way or another, their fears do become yours.

Their fears don't have to stay your fears; as I've said, none of us is so weak that we have no choice but to become junior versions of our parents. But we all carry within us the emotional legacy that our parents couldn't help but bequeath to us, and part of the challenge we all face in life is to overcome the parts of that legacy that either aren't really natural to us or that are flat-out bad for us to continue having to carry.

Another word for the totality of the negative emotional weight we all inherit is *baggage*. I love that use of that word; *baggage* is exactly how that part of our parents' psychologies feels. What we received that burdens us throughout our own lives feels like extra weight we're carrying around (and very often, of course, is).

If we're going to have productive relationships that lead to a regret-free life, we must learn to drop our unwanted baggage. As anyone knows who has ever flown in those soaring sardine cans they call airplanes, baggage does nothing so much as get in the way and cramp everybody's style. And anything extra makes for hassle and inconvenience.

Below are some ways to help you get rid of extra baggage so that you can finally upgrade your life from coach to first class.

Unpacking Your Baggage

I've spoken a bit about what is meant here by *baggage*, how that word refers to the amalgam of unhealthy and/or unhelpful attitudes and beliefs we inherited from our parents. We all have baggage; we all know we have baggage; most of us understand that our baggage constitutes much of what's standing between us and the regret-free living we know God would have us live.

The question for most of us is, what's *in* our baggage? What exactly are we carrying around? Why is it so heavy? And why (as long as we're asking all the big questions here) does it seem to so often change shape on us? Why can't our personal, emotional baggage ever be like real luggage—definite, manageable, something that we can choose to grasp, understand, and unpack whenever and however we want to.

Because that's really what it's all about, isn't it: unpacking our baggage. Learning how is one of the biggest challenges of our lives. If we could do that—if we could figure out what part of us is good, permanent, real, and helpful, and get rid of all the stuff in our hearts and minds that is the opposite of those things—we could finally be the person we know inside we were born to be. That's what each of us intuits, and we're right. To a large degree, our baggage really is simply weighing us down.

If we could just unpack our baggage, put away into the neat drawers of our hearts and minds everything we know we could use on our trip through life, and throw away the broken bottles and wadded-up papers that never should have been packed in the first place, we'd be a lot happier and healthier.

And yet . . . the zipper on that piece of our luggage is forever getting stuck. Or we get *some* of that bag unpacked—and then, somehow, something new and awful ends up back inside it, and we find that it's managed to become zipped up again. And maybe this time there's a padlock on the zipper. Or maybe the whole thing has been wrapped in duct tape. Or rope. Or maybe the suitcase has been dipped in resin and is now as hard as stone.

For most of us, unpacking our baggage becomes simply too difficult. So rather than try, we fling the thing over our shoulder, bend our back a bit in response to the weight, and keep on trudging forward.

But Christians are not burdened as others are. What is impossible for people is nothing to the Lord. Yes, the weight is heavy; yes, the weight of the baggage causes strain. But with God lending us a helping hand and showing us the way, we need not struggle at all.

It's not necessarily the easiest thing to do, but what we must do if we want to live our life free of our baggage's weight is call upon God to ease our burden. We have no other choice; no human really does.

We can pretend we're capable of relieving ourselves of our heavy load, but we're not. We can and must do a lot of the work ourselves; I know there's a great deal each of us must do if we want to prepare the way for the Lord to do the rest. And we will spend the rest of this book talking about what we can and must do to help ourselves. But ultimately—once we've done all we can—we will have to come before the Lord, fall to our knees, and ask for

DROPPING YOUR BAGGAGE   // 125

his help in eradicating from our heart and soul what we can be relieved of *only* by his loving grace.

Let's do what we can—and then, fully prepared, let's go before the Lord and beseech him to do what we cannot.

> *Come to me, all of you who are weary and carry heavy burdens, and I will give you rest. Take my yoke upon you. Let me teach you, because I am humble and gentle at heart, and you will find rest for your souls. For my yoke is easy to bear, and the burden I give you is light.* (Matthew 11:28–30)

Onward!

Who Packed Your Stuff, Anyway?

Through the years I have learned much about treating clients who are burdened with psychological disorders. One of the most important things I've learned is that there's no single better way for me to quickly gain insight into the particular challenges of a particular person than to meet his or her parents.

I could have worked with someone any number of times in a treatment center. I could have had them in my office for uninterrupted hours of conversation. I could have spent hours upon hours of my own private time thinking about and analyzing their problems. I could have applied every therapeutic method I know to them and their concerns—and none of it will bring me the knowledge about that person that I'll gain through just one meeting with their parents.

With one of their parents, I'll draw very close to the core of their problem. If I meet both parents, I'll practically know them better than they know themselves.

Of course, there's often a problem. The people who need the most help are least likely to be in much touch with their parents at all.

Remember Tolstoy's words about how all dysfunctional families are dysfunctional in a way totally unique to them? That's true, but in the end you can apply at least one rule to a great many dysfunctional families: Its members barely ever talk to each other.

Such a distressingly large number of families, when their children come of age, utterly shatter, with its members either moving as far away as possible or burying themselves so deeply in their own lives that they never make any time for the other relatives. Sometimes I even hate asking a client, "Do you often see or speak to your family members?" because I fear I already know the answer. I can almost always tell when the answer is going to be that they don't. Frequently, people who give that answer are some of the most troubled people I see.

As helpful as it is being able to meet the parents of someone who's come to me, it's also true that I can almost always tell much about a person's parents just by spending enough time listening to them talk about their life and problems. Parents create a kind of psychic imprint upon the minds and souls of their children, and it directly reflects the entirety of their own psyches.

It's like Silly Putty. (Remember Silly Putty? They still make that stuff!) It's soft; it's malleable; if you press it up against an image and then peel it back off again, that image, if slightly attenuated, will be on it.

Parents are the original image; their children are the Silly Putty. (Which perhaps helps explain why, when I was a kid, I used to spend so much time bouncing around. Which is a comment you won't understand if you've never played with Silly Putty. . . .)

The kind of baggage we're talking about here has a strange quality to it. You can't unpack it until you know who packed it in the first place.

And that road always leads back to the same place: Mom and Dad.

They packed it; we carry it. This makes our world go round.

And it's also, I think, a large part of the truth Jesus was getting at when he said what has since caused so many followers so much wonder:

If anyone comes to me and does not hate his father and mother, his wife and children, his brothers and sisters—yes, even his own life—he cannot be my disciple. (Luke 14:26 NIV)

It could be that Jesus isn't telling us to hate our parents. He's telling us to hate what we inherited that keeps us from living fully with him. For one thing, he's saying that if we have to choose between what our parents "taught" us and what he wants to teach us, we take our lessons from him.

Leaving Behind What's Weighing You Down

Leaving behind the weight is just about the most exciting thing you can think about doing, isn't it? Is there anything we'd like to do more than finally, once and for all, leave behind everything that's draining us?

That's what all people want! Freedom!

The interesting thing about "leaving" our baggage behind is that it means doing the opposite of what we usually think when regarding leaving anything behind. Usually, it means walking away from it. But not your baggage. *The only way to truly, effectively, and permanently leave behind everything that's psychologically weighing you down is to walk not only toward it but into it.*

You have to dismantle what's holding you back. The only way to do it is to delve into its innermost workings. You must roll up your sleeves, find an entranceway, move into it, and start taking it apart.

In the end it's not about walking away from anything. The idea of walking away from something is you leave that thing as it is; you simply leave or abandon it. But it doesn't work that way with psychological or spiritual issues. You can't walk away from something that by definition follows you everywhere you go. Trying to walk away from baggage is like trying to walk away from ears or arms. You can't. It's part of you.

What you *can* do with baggage, though, is understand it. It's through understanding a thing that it ceases to hold its power over us—that's when it ceases to be a mystery to us. It's the mysterious that grips us, that frightens us, that seems beyond our ability to control or resist it. Remember *The Wizard of Oz*? Remember how awesome and frightening the wizard was—right up until the moment when Toto pulled aside the curtain to reveal the real "wizard," who proved to be nothing more than an unremarkable man?

That's when the wizard stopped being such a fearsome power; indeed, that's when he lost virtually all power to influence or affect anyone at all.

The baggage we carry around is the wizard of our Oz. It seems too terrible to resist, too powerful for us to conquer. We don't know anything about anyone hiding behind any curtain; all we know is that the thing we're trying to fight always beats us in the end.

So we fear it. So we dream of walking away from it.

Well, no more. If we want to lead a regret-free life, we must stop thinking there's anything in our mind, or any influence from our past, that we cannot, with God's loving help, grasp and conquer.

Make a list of what you think your biggest problems are, of what you think is inside that baggage that's weighing you down.

And then, one by one, pray about these things. Ask God to absolutely and finally deliver you from them. Ask him to show you what they really are so that, demystified, they finally can lose their grip on you.

Before praying about any of the items in your baggage, be sure to read and reflect upon Romans 8:31–39:

> *If God is for us, who can ever be against us? Since he did not spare even his own Son but gave him up for us all, won't he also give us everything else? Who dares accuse us whom God has chosen for his own? No one—for God himself has given us right standing with himself. Who then will condemn us? No one—for Christ Jesus died for us and was raised to life for us, and he is sitting in the place of honor at God's right hand, pleading for us.*
>
> *Can anything ever separate us from Christ's love? Does it mean he no longer loves us if we have trouble or calamity, or are persecuted, or hungry, or destitute, or in danger, or threatened with death? (As the Scriptures say, "For your sake we are killed*

every day; we are being slaughtered like sheep.") No, despite all these things, overwhelming victory is ours through Christ, who loved us.

And I am convinced that nothing can ever separate us from God's love. Neither death nor life, neither angels nor demons, neither our fears for today nor our worries about tomorrow—not even the powers of hell can separate us from God's love. No power in the sky above or in the earth below—indeed, nothing in all creation will ever be able to separate us from the love of God that is revealed in Christ Jesus our Lord.

The Joy of Dropping Your Heavy Load

One time a woman came to me who I could tell was going to have a real challenge getting from where she was (and had been) to where she wanted to be. She was a statuesque and truly beautiful woman, and it was no stretch at all to believe that "Allison" had been the model she claimed she'd been.

She had a fair number of psychological problems, but the one that most concerned me was how dysfunctionally she treated her two children. At that time her boys were eleven and thirteen, and without going into detail, suffice it to say that she was failing in her efforts to properly raise them after having divorced their father.

Things in the life of Allison and her sons were becoming really desperate. Her boys were spending a lot more time—and, increasingly, a lot more nights—away from their home than any kid their age ever should. They were beginning to dabble in drugs; they were hanging around with an older gang of kids who, safe to say, didn't exactly have their best interests at heart. They'd been in serious trouble at school; twice they'd been delivered home by police. Their future was looking increasingly dim; they were going nowhere, but fast.

As disturbing as all this was, Allison apparently was disinterested in their lives and fortunes. Even though of course she was aware of what was happening, she had utterly surrounded herself with a façade of hardened disinterest.

"They're almost fully grown," she said from behind the large sunglasses she always wore. "There's nothing I can do with them. They're like their father—determined to do whatever they want, however they want, to whomever they want. It's not my problem. I've done what I can."

I decided to dedicate a lot of time to Allison; I'd met her two boys and, despite their studied air of cynicism and callousness, liked them very much. I wanted them to be okay. I knew they wouldn't be if something radical with their mom didn't change.

The more I came to know about Allison, the more I became distressed over her past, which was as difficult as any I've yet to hear. I won't go into details, but let's just say that Allison's having started her life as a dirt-poor orphan in the woods of the Deep South was the least of her problems growing up.

It's just amazing what some people endure.

But of course her past had taken a toll—a toll that her children were now paying with their lives.

The more I got to know Allison, the more I began to see that her issues boiled down to the same basic dynamic: Her parents had adopted her out of the conviction that bringing this adorable little girl into their lives would solve all the terrible problems in their marriage. And when that didn't work, what do you think happened?

They blamed their newer, deeper misery on their innocent little girl.

That, for Allison, is when things started going from bad to worse.

Eventually, in her talks with me, Allison saw (all in one of those wonderfully cataclysmic breakthrough moments that people serious about looking at their pasts are sometimes blessed to experience) that her parents had blamed her for their unhappiness, for not saving them.

And once she understood that, the sun started shining again in her life. Suddenly she understood that there was nothing wrong with her. She wasn't cursed with something that made her unlovable. She wasn't bad. She wasn't wrong.

She'd been wronged.

Within a mere month of her understanding that the load she'd been burdened with all her life wasn't hers but belonged instead to her poor adoptive parents, Allison's life had completely turned around. She joined a church. She got very involved in her sons' lives—but in a loving, nurturing way that brought them back to her, that got them once again interested in their own lives. She even picked up again a love of hers that she'd long since let go, playing the piano.

Everything changed when Allison realized how to let go of what, in the end, she discovered was never hers in the first place.

And just like that, Allison's life went from broken to joyous.

The joy of dropping your heavy load is that it frees you to become the person that God and you—whether or not, at any given time of your life, you know it—most want you to be.

"The truth will set you free" (John 8:32). And it's in this freedom that we finally find the joy Jesus wants us to know and have and share.

The Cost of Traveling Light

The cost of continuing your life after you've managed to let go of the baggage that's long been weighing you down is this: *To a large degree the whole script of your post-baggage life must be rewritten.* To a degree you can barely begin to understand until you've experienced it firsthand, everything you are—your persona, your idea of yourself, the "you" you've learned to be while doing whatever it is you do—is gone once you've lost the baggage you've been carrying so long that it defines much of you.

Losing your baggage isn't like getting a new haircut or buying a cool new wardrobe. It's a constitutional restructure. It means everything in your life has changed.

The problem with this—the cost that it inevitably means you have to pay—is that while everything on the inside of you changes, nothing in the outside world changes at all. Your spouse remains the same. Your children continue to be the same. Your parents remain the same people who raised you. Your boss, as ever, stubbornly refuses to change. Your colleagues change in no discernable way. Your neighbors continue to play their stereo too loud or mow their lawn too early.

You're different—but no one else is.

This certainly is not as much of a problem as was carrying around that baggage in the first place. But the new challenges that come with traveling light can prove to be uniquely challenging in their own right. In fact, they can be so difficult that they end up becoming a whole new set of baggage you end up carrying before you even realize it's strapped to your back. No matter how definitively you've changed, the people about whom you care the most, by sheer force of habit as much as by anything else, essentially will insist that you continue being for them the same person you always have been. They like you the way you *used* to be—even though it might seem like they wouldn't. They like you the way you were back when you were traveling heavy instead of light, because that's how they know you. That's how they're accustomed to you.

And you (for better or worse) love those nearest to you just the way *they* are too. This isn't something that changes when you drop your baggage; if anything, you then love them more than you ever did, insofar as your opened heart allows you to see their flaws less as affronts than as indicators of their broken humanness. *We are never so loving toward others as when we have learned to be loving toward ourselves.*

And it's because of the love you feel for those nearest you that you are entirely likely to want to become again for them what you have always been. They will want you to become again the enabling spouse, the self-sacrificing sibling, the pliant employee, the too-busy-to-care parent. And that is something you must resist, for your good and theirs. As you have, in effect, been reprogrammed according to the new life-design God has revealed to you, so in turn you must reprogram those nearest you to change the way they see and interact with you.

That's the real price of traveling light: this new line you have to continuously draw for those who might not be used to you having any lines at all. Nevertheless, you must put forth that effort—you must insist that you really are who you're really becoming—because failing to do so makes certain that you will end up creating new regrets. It means exchanging what God gave you for what you already had—which is to say, for something less than what God gave you. And we always regret choosing anything but the love God is constantly offering us.

The cost of traveling light is to never allow yourself to waver from the truth expressed by Jesus:

> *"Anyone who listens to my teaching and follows it is wise, like a person who builds a house on solid rock. Though the rain comes in torrents and the floodwaters rise and the winds beat against that house, it won't collapse because it is built on bedrock. But anyone who hears my teaching and doesn't obey it is foolish, like a person who builds a house on sand. When the rains and floods come and the winds beat against that house, it will collapse with a mighty crash."*
>
> *When Jesus had finished saying these things, the crowds were amazed at his teaching, for he taught with real authority—quite unlike their teachers of religious law.* (Matthew 7:24–29)

CHAPTER 8

When It's Time
to Pack Up and Leave

A friend of mine, whom I'll call Jill, once opened up a beauty salon with a woman I'll call Clara. They each put a lot of money into their new business and were excited about it. They opened in a perfect location, right on the main drag of the kind of California coastal town where many wealthy women spend much on shopping, lunching, and deciding they have just enough time to stop in and get their hair done.

At first, everything about Jill and Clara's business seemed to thrive. They found excellent cosmetologists to rent their stations, and good word-of-mouth about their salon began to spread. They had their problems, as all new businesses do, but it seemed clear to them that their gamble of shared partnership was going to pay off.

About six months in, though, Jill began to notice that Clara spent more and more time away from the salon. And, increasingly, the time Clara did spend at work was less and less productive. It appeared to Jill that the more successful the business grew, the more Clara seemed to disengage from all the work and decision-making Jill knew was necessary to ensure its ongoing success.

When Jill tried to talk with Clara about her concern, Clara's initial response was "What are you worried about? We're doing great! The place runs itself!" This alarmed Jill; the salon did not, in fact, run itself at all—it was just that more and more Jill was the one running it.

Over the following months, Clara's attitude grew to where she was having almost nothing to do with the day-to-day operation. Now, she was *there* a lot; she loved hanging out with the beauticians and the customers. But when it came to handling the books or dealing with the paper work, Clara was a partner *non grata*.

Jill grew increasingly apprehensive about her relationship with Clara. They were friends; they'd known each other for years. But she was finding their new shared path to be more and more unstable.

"I need help with the business," she said. Clara agreed to resume pitching in and doing more, and she did . . . for about four days.

"We're supposed to be partners, Clara," Jill said. "It's not right for you to leave me to do all the real work of this place." And so again Clara agreed to start pulling her weight . . . and then again failed to do so.

Jill talked with Clara again and again. And again. She pleaded. She prayed. She sought counsel from others. She was as honest, loving, thoughtful, and respectful as she knew how to be. In the end, it got her nothing; all Clara seemed to know how to do was *say* she was getting the message and *say* she meant to start working to uphold the salon.

In the end, each time Clara's words proved to be nothing more.

Finally there came a point where Jill had to admit to herself that they simply couldn't continue to be business partners.

"I give up," she said, in tears, one night to her husband. "I can't make this work with Clara. There's nothing more I can do; no other approach I can think of or haven't tried. She's just not going to participate in what we're supposed to be doing together."

Later Jill told me:

Once I realized that my relationship with Clara was never going to work, I felt this huge weight lifting off my shoulder. It changed everything. All of a sudden, all the burden I'd been saddled with—all this emotional grief, anxiety, and anger I'd been wrestling with so long—vanished. I had tried my best, ten times over. I knew that was all I could do. And I knew that, as painful as it was to contemplate, it was time for Clara and me to dissolve our professional relationship. I'd had enough. It was over.

Jill's decision to formally separate from Clara didn't come easy—it had a very high cost (both figuratively and literally). Ultimately, though, she did the only thing she could do if she wanted to move on with her life. She declared herself independent of her erstwhile partner, and she moved on. No matter how tough, it was the right choice.

■ ■ ■

As we've been seeing all along, a huge part of living regret-free is learning to make and carry through with important personal decisions. Often that's not particularly easy or fun to do, but if you've been shown by the Lord and your experience that an avenue is the right one for you to travel down, then taking control of your life so that you can live regret-free means that you have to strap on your shoes and get hiking.

We can't shirk from our responsibilities and at the same time avoid the results of what happens when we do. If God clearly and firmly points the way to us, we have no choice but to go that way. Going any other way is what leads us inevitably to regrets.

One of the most difficult decisions any of us ever has to make is to finally end it with another person. Nothing's more painful than having to conclude that despite all the care, love, patience, and understanding you've poured into a relationship—despite everything you've done—it simply cannot be saved.

We tend to continue to believe that relationships we want to work out can work out, even long after anyone else looking on from the outside would readily see that it's just never going to work. The main reason most of us persevere in a bad relationship is that we love the other person and don't want to let them go. So we keep trying and trying and trying, and giving and giving, hoping against hope that he or she finally will hear what we're saying, think about what we're asking, understand where we're coming from.

And sometimes, no matter what we say—no matter how many talks we initiate, letters we write, phone calls we make, counseling sessions we go to, or prayers we send to God—the relationship still doesn't work. Until finally, we have to admit that we've run out of options, that it will never, ever work.

What do we do then? What should our attitude be toward those difficult relationships that we can tell are never going to succeed?

Well, we have three choices. We can either, as they say, grin and bear it, we can work to improve it, or we can choose to make a final and definitive break.

It's the latter choice that we're going to discuss in this chapter. From here on out we're going to assume that we're talking about a relationship you can no longer simply "grin and bear." And there are very few, if any, relationships in our lives that we must approach in that way. If a relationship is truly toxic—if the other person is just too abusive—then you have to find safety. It's certainly not God's heart for you to continue in a relationship where you have been abandoned and abused and betrayed.

God loves you and wants you to be fulfilled. And if ultimately that means breaking off an important relationship you've tried your very best to reconcile and heal, then sometimes, with God's help and guidance, packing up may be the best thing you can do.

That's never an easy thing to do, of course. And if the relationship that's not working for you is with your spouse, then you should do every last thing you can—and a whole lot more after that—before you even think whether it is appropriate for you to get a divorce. *That* should be a decision made every bit as carefully as should the decision to get married. Divorce is a life-scarring tragedy, and no one should go into it lightly or under the wrong circumstances.

But sometimes, as happened in my life, it happens to you. It's not your choice.

■   ■   ■

Let's talk about the process of breaking up, which at first might seem intimidating and difficult but ultimately can be as freeing and inspiring as anything you've ever had the strength to do for yourself.

Recognizing the Signs

Not too long ago I was tooling around the hills of Los Angeles in a sports car that I was enjoying very much. Low to the ground; power like a rocket ship; handled like . . . well, like an expensive sports car. That automobile had everything a middle-aged man could ask for, and more. I was in cruising heaven.

I was driving on Sunset Boulevard, nearly blinded by the setting sun, the general direction toward which I was heading. As happens with winding roads, sometimes I'd be staring directly toward the sun, sometimes it would be on my left or right side, and sometimes I'd catch a break and find myself zipping along in nothing but cool California shade.

Then, suddenly, I realized I was probably about to enter, in a most gruesome fashion, the heaven that isn't metaphorical at all. I was going to die!

I'd just come around a corner onto what I saw as a clear, fairly long stretch of road. Glad to finally have a moment in which I didn't have to execute yet another turn, I gunned the car a little bit. The sun was gleaming through my windshield, so I didn't have a perfectly clear view, but I could see far enough ahead to think I could finally stretch the car.

Wrong. As it turned out, that little span of road was exactly long enough for a person to get up to forty or so miles an hour (easy, in a car like I was driving), and short enough to kill that person once he realized it ended in an extremely sharp turn that, if carelessly navigated, guaranteed a plunge into a valley floor so far down a guy couldn't hold his breath as long as he fell.

Not good.

And right at the beginning of the sharp turn away from Death Plunge—actually into the turn a bit—was a little yellow sign humbly proclaiming "25 MPH." Twenty-five! At the very end of one big road tease.

Into the sun, a radically sharp turn after a straight stretch, a tiny sign, and a deep, deep plunge. Quite the killer combo. Truly, as it turned out. When I later found out how many people have died on that very turn, I can't say I was surprised. I was just glad I was not among them. And a good deal gladder for exactly how well that car handled.

That, more than any other sort of warning or signal system, is what it's often like when we finally realize a relationship really and truly isn't ever going to work. The truth of it can just suddenly be there, waiting for us to crash into it. Even though we know we've been taking lots of turns this way and that, sometimes it's the finality of what we've come to that's so suddenly upon us.

And we don't want this to happen. Though on the literal road in my story there weren't enough needful signs leading up to the potential crash site, you can trust there are signs leading up to a relational dead end.

The other person never really finishes a conversation with you; they always storm out, get too upset to continue, never listen, or always have to take a call. But always, they make sure the conversation stops.

They won't take your efforts to heal with them seriously. They belittle your attempts to emotionally bond with them. They won't acknowledge the validity of your needs and desires. They pretend they can't understand what you want—and then, when they do understand perfectly well, they continuously and purposefully thwart your plans and desires. They won't stick to what they've said; trying to get them to commit to a plan or idea is like trying to hold on to sand.

Mostly, they won't change. That's really the sign that you're dealing with someone it's probably best to move on without. It often takes a while before you come to see that he or she is forever going to insist on remaining exactly as difficult as they've always been. But once that fact sinks in, it changes the rules of your approach. Usually, it means your choice is simple: Keep taking the only thing they're giving, or move on.

Knowing You've Done What You Can

One of the keys—in a lot of ways the only key—to a regret-free life is knowing, at every moment along the way, that you've done everything you can. That's how you lay your head on your pillow at night and sleep what the sages have long called "the sleep of the innocent." You achieve peace—by day or by night—by actually being innocent.

Availing ourselves of God's redemptive power through the sacrifice of his Son for our sins is, of course, the efficacious means for returning to a God-blessed innocence. Our sin is washed clean in Christ's blood; we ask for his forgiveness, and our wholeness, or innocence, is returned to us. This divine forgiveness—this means by which anyone can truly be born again—is the greatest gift God has given to all of humankind.

But God's offering does not mean that literally all we have to do in order to be good and true followers is, at the end of every day, fall to our knees and seek forgiveness. That won't do. We have personal responsibilities to do what we can to make manifest the very love that God brought to us through his incarnation as Jesus.

Moved by the power of Jesus' story and the Holy Spirit within us, we seek to be as much like him as possible. This is our duty in life as followers of Christ. And it means that we must take care, every minute of every hour of every day of our lives, to simply and utterly do everything we can to make God proud.

■ ■ ■

When dealing with a relationship that we're beginning to see is beyond our power to redeem, the first thing we must do before deciding is to make sure that we can tell ourselves—and thereby also tell the Spirit within us, which (let us never forget) is God himself—that we have done everything we can to save that relationship. In all honesty, we have to be able to say that we have given (metaphorically) nothing less than what God, through Jesus, gave us. Jesus spared no pain to himself in order to assure we could be fully justified before God; we, then, must also give our all to somebody that God has seen fit to put into our lives.

Your spouse. Your parents. Your siblings. Your friends. Your co-workers. Your neighbors. Your children. These are our most important relationships. If your relationship with one such person has gone so awry that you've finally reached the point where you know your ties must be permanently severed, then it's absolutely essential, before you in any way formally separate, that you do a thorough and brutally honest assessment, and make sure that you find nothing in the relationship's history that will lead to your later being burdened with regrets over how you handled any aspect of it.

Have you given the other person a chance to talk with you, to say what they wanted to say, as many times as they wanted, uninterrupted? Have you listened—really listened? Have you tried to do things their way? Have you initiated the exchanges, made the phone calls, written the letters and e-mails, made the personal visits? Have you kept the peace?

Have you, in short, treated them the way that God, through Jesus, has treated you?

Pray about this. Take the time that breaking up with someone should take, so that you can properly reflect upon what you're about to do. Severing a relationship that God has put in your life is a matter very near to the heart of the Prince of Peace. Don't take it lightly.

But if, in the final analysis—after you've prayed about it, after you've sought the counsel of loved ones, after you've spent all the time and energy necessary to know in your heart of hearts that you've done everything to salvage and heal the relationship—you still know that you have to break with the other person, then move toward doing that.

God grieves over every soul that chooses hell over him. But people do make that choice. When they do, God has no choice but to separate them forever from his presence.

Sadly, sometimes we too must banish someone from our own love. But just like it's not God's fault that any given person chooses hell, it's not your fault if someone has forced you to let go of them. God is honoring a person's free will when he allows them to separate themselves from him. You likewise are honoring the other person's free will if, time and time again, they have proven that they don't want to be with you in a way that would be pleasing to God.

If you know you've done everything you can to produce a healthy relationship, and he or she has refused that gift, then just like God must turn from those who refuse the gift of his love, so you have to turn away from those who refuse the gift of yours. You can do so knowing that, since breaking up was ultimately their choice, you'll never have anything to regret about that decision.

Making the Break

Obviously, how you go about finally and definitively "breaking up" depends upon who you are and the nature of the relationship. If the person with whom you're separating is your boss at work, then "breaking up" might mean nothing more dramatic or personal than simply looking for and taking a different job. In that case, your big good-bye need be nothing much more than a two-week notice and a handshake.

It's not usually that easy, though, is it? If it's a spouse or family member with whom you simply can't find a way to relate healthily, then clearly defining the new limits you would like to impose can be a tricky, emotional kind of ride. You can say you're no longer going to be around your father so that he doesn't keep emotionally abusing you—but then what are you going to do about that big annual family Thanksgiving dinner? You can determine you're never going to be able to make it fly with a professional associate—but if you're not in a position to fire that person, what are you going to do the next day at work or with the next project on which you're supposed to work together?

There are really only two ways to go about finalizing your break. You either tell that person the reason you're breaking up with them, or you don't. Which option you choose relative to any given person will depend upon what necessarily happens with that person after you've broken with them. If they're not going to be in your life thereafter, or if you can definitely arrange it so that they won't be in your life anymore following the break, then you can and perhaps even should tell them why you've finally given up on ever having a healthy relationship with them.

The other kind of breakup is where you break up with the person in your heart but do not share with them the matter of having arrived at the conclusion that it's hopeless. It's a breakup you keep to yourself. This is usually the way you have to handle a final separation from someone with whom you will or might continue contact. This is where you continue, because you must, interacting with the other person, but do not continue, because you needn't, believing in a productive future with that person. This is the kind of break largely defined by how differently you *feel* toward the other person, if not how you actually *act*. It's where, instead of emotionally engaging, you emotionally detach.

A third way—which is really just a subset of the second way— is where you simply let a relationship peter out. You do nothing to keep it going. You don't return the phone calls, you ignore e-mails, you keep being too busy to meet for lunch or dinner. Pretty soon the other person gets the hint and, voilà, they're out of your life. This is the style so many young women employ when they're dating. It's like poking a tiny hole in a big balloon. Eventually, it simply deflates and floats back down to earth. No harm, no foul.

Whichever way circumstances dictate that you handle your breakup, be sure to *always handle yourself with dignity*. People's feelings will be at stake, and so in the final exchanges wherein you set the new parameters, be sure to never give yourself any reason to later regret anything you said or did. When you're breaking up with someone, you're also creating memories that will probably last for the rest of your lives. If there's ever a time to act right, it's then. Remember that God is watching and listening to everything you do and say. Make him proud.

Owning What You've Learned

Any important, long-term relationship is like a diamond. The pressure put upon it eventually turns it into something of true value that you can really use to enhance your life in just about any way you want.

When before the break you've spent significant time and energy trying to reconcile with another person, you've learned something—much, in fact—from that relationship. It usually doesn't feel like that, especially the closer you are to the time of the actual break. Usually, right then you feel like the entire thing was a giant waste of your time.

"Look at everything I gave to him/her," we complain. "Look at all the time I gave. Look at how hard I worked on making it work. Look at how much this relationship cost me. And what was it all for? Nothing! It was a complete loss."

But it wasn't. It never is. It's just that sometimes it takes a while after a relationship has dissolved for us to understand all the good it's actually done for us. Take Alka-Seltzer. You drop it in the water. It fizzes and foams and causes all kinds of commotion inside the glass—and then it all calms down, and you drink it, and pretty soon you feel better.

Same with a relationship we're ending. At first, once we've dropped it into the water of the breakup, the relationship is very tumultuous, popping and making all kinds of noise, being almost frighteningly active. But later, once everything has calmed down and things have resumed their more natural place and rhythm, you can begin to experience how beneficial the whole of that relationship has been to you. You begin to see how much you learned from it, how much you grew because of it. You begin to understand how much better your next relationship like it will be, because of everything you have learned from failure.

If after you've broken up with someone you find yourself not at all feeling like you've gained a great deal from your past experiences with him or her—if once it's ended you're left feeling less like you're holding a sparkling diamond and more like it's a plain chunk of coal—then you're not giving yourself or your experience anywhere near enough credit.

As sure as the earth goes round the sun, you did learn something. In a way that nothing else could have taught you, because nothing else would have involved you as much, you learned about your weaknesses, your strengths, your power to endure, your abilities to reassess, reinvigorate, reorganize, reorient. You learned what buttons someone else can push, and how. You learned what makes you act childish, what makes you act noble, what leaves you wondering how you're supposed to act. You learned the role time can play in letting things work out; you learned how and when to preempt time's effects, shaping things into what you know it's best they become.

In a nutshell, you learned a lot about not only who you have been and who you are, but also who you can become.

God doesn't bring difficult relationships into our lives so that we can waste our time and learn nothing from them. It is easy enough to continue on with someone and not really learn much. Those kinds of relationships—the pleasant-enough kind we typically enjoy with co-workers or neighbors—are perfectly fine and even necessary; we all have many in our lives. But consider that a challenging relationship you've ultimately had to dissolve was brought to you by God as a means of his teaching you some very specific lessons.

As you move ahead after you've broken up, be sure to make a point of regularly sitting down, closing your eyes, and listening to what God would like to teach you about that relationship. And then, armed with what you've learned about how to most productively engage with others, move forward and begin living your new God-blessed, regret-free life.

CHAPTER 9

Creating a Safety Zone

Jeff hadn't seen or talked to his brother, Paul, in more than fifteen years. Growing up they had endured the usual sibling rivalry, but theirs had lasted longer than usual. They didn't get along as children; they didn't get along as teenagers; and they didn't get along as adults. Mostly, as adults, they never spoke to each other.

And then Jeff began to realize he was missing something in his life without his brother being part of it. He especially began to feel it when their sister, Angela, was diagnosed with cancer. Sitting with Angela as she went through and recovered from chemotherapy (she's now cancer-free!), Jeff began to feel that just as he was holding his sister's hand, in his other he should be holding his brother's. They should be together at their sister's side. Beyond that, they should be together in life.

Finally, Jeff decided to call his brother. *Enough,* he thought, *is enough.*

Paul wasn't as happy to get the call as Jeff hoped he would be. He wasn't completely cold, but he didn't sound too interested in getting together either. A lot of the old grievances between them were still very much alive, at least in one of their hearts.

I met with Jeff between the time he had arranged to get together with his brother and the time they actually met. When Jeff asked me what I thought would be the best way to prepare for his upcoming meeting, I gave him the same advice I'd like to share with you now.

■　■　■

It's one thing to make peace with someone with whom you've been warring. It's a big thing too; as we know and have seen, replacing war with love takes a major amount of effort, time, patience, and allowing God to pick up where you necessarily leave off. It's no mean feat.

The question we'll examine now is, what do you do once you've succeeded at *reconnecting* with someone with whom you've long been *disconnected*? Once you've gotten someone you haven't eaten with in a long time to sit down again with you and enjoy a meal—to sip wine with you, to enjoy food with you, to relax in your company and again share joy and laughter—then what? What happens after you're done with that wonderful reconciliatory meal? What happens once the table has been cleared, once the dishes have all been washed and put away, once it's time for you and your beloved guest to go your separate ways?

How do you keep something going that of its own accord must sooner or later end?

How, in other words, do you keep the peace once you've made it?

I recommend creating what I call a "safety zone." I'm very keen on the idea that any two people, just like nations, can agree on a space between them wherein no demonstrations of hostility are allowed. A safety zone, whether it be between countries or individuals, represents a place where pure, peaceful nature exists, and nothing else. No firearms. No land mines. No jets overhead. Nothing but good ol' peace and quiet.

If people groups that have been at war can have clearly defined safety or peaceful zones established between them, the neutrality of which both parties pre-agree to honor and maintain, then I see no reason why individuals who have been at war can't establish the same kind of demilitarized zone.

One of the greatest gifts of living in Christ is that I'm never as smart today as I will be tomorrow. How can I be, when at every moment he's teaching me? I once thought the only way to create a space between me and someone with whom I was having difficulties was to create as much actual distance as possible. My way of coping with stressful relational periods used to be to literally fly away. There was always somewhere for me to go, something for me to do, some business somewhere that needed my attention.

In the family setting, all along what I should have been doing was staying home and embracing the conflict, living in it so that its issues would finally be resolved. I didn't need to get on a plane to feel safe in the midst of a struggle. I could have stayed and created a zone for managing the heat of the moment.

Let's look at how you can do the same between you and anyone you've been battling.

Writing a Peace Treaty

I may be more biased toward this opinion than the average person (in fact, given that I've written over eighty books, it's a guarantee), but I believe great things can be done through the written word. Of course, we already know that; every day (hopefully) we take deep pleasure and find true spiritual inspiration and succor in the very word of God. And of course the power of words hardly stops there; in every facet of the human experience, from law to medicine to history to literature, the written word is foundation, dressing, and crowning achievement.

But the written word can be used in our private, personal lives with all the impact and import it so often carries in our public, corporate lives. I have always been a big fan of the personal mission statement. Most of us have by now heard of the business mission statement, which results from the leaders of a company or organization first thinking long and hard about its true values, purpose, and goals—and then taking the time to carefully articulate them in a succinct, clear statement.

That sentence or two then becomes the mission statement, which, ideally, is regularly used to remind employees and associates of what that company is, what it stands for, and what it's striving to achieve every day. It's easy enough to take a company's mission statement for granted—to see it, if at all, as just another posting on the lunchroom bulletin board, or just another poster in the waiting room—but the head of any company who allows the mission statement to become merely another easily overlooked platitude is missing a fantastic opportunity to constantly promote and keep alive everything that should be making the company stand out and excel. A mission statement shouldn't be a static, stale thing; it should be dynamic, vital . . . as alive as alive gets.

We worked very hard, for instance, formulating the mission statement for New Life Ministries: "To identify and compassionately respond to the needs of those seeking healing and restoration through God's truth." There. That's what New Life is; that's what New Life does. And it's the first thing people see when they go to the "About Us" page on *www.newlife.com*. I'm proud of our mission statement and even prouder of the people who put its ideals into action every day.

So it's really a combination—as all good mission statements are—of values and goals that are both personal and public. But I believe it can be taken to an even more intimate level. I believe each person, in their own time and way, would be wise to write for themselves a mission statement capturing who they are, what they value, and what they stand for in life.

(Imagine everyone walking around wearing a T-shirt with his or her personal mission statement on it. You could look at one person and say, "Oh, she lives for honesty and integrity." Hopefully you wouldn't see, "He believes it's better to punch first and ask questions later!")

Try it yourself. Write a mission statement, saying who you are, what you believe in, what you stand for, what you hope to accomplish. Make it positive, simple, and brief. Three to five sentences should do it. Take your time with it too. It typically takes months for a company that's taking it seriously to arrive at its perfected mission statement. You don't have to take that long, of course, but don't rush it. Think about it. Look at other mission statements. Pray about it. Let it come to you.

Once it has, and you've created a mission statement that you're confident fully captures you and your ideals, use it as a tool in establishing and keeping the peace with anyone in your life with whom you want to take the time and effort to do that blessed work. I'll show you what I mean.

Establishing the Peace

In a very important sense, a personal mission statement is to a person what a constitution is to a whole country. A constitution is a people's core-identifying document, the main body of thought that must be taken into account whenever one is in any official capacity to deal with that country. Just like a personal mission statement tells anyone who reads it all they really need to know about the person who wrote it, a constitution tells the world everything it really needs to know about the foundational values and goals of the country that produced it.

Creating a constitution is one of the most important steps a new nation can take in its efforts to be recognized as legitimate. It must have a constitution—it must clearly identify itself in that way—before it can move on to the other business that any people naturally undertakes.

And now that you have your "personal constitution," you can move on to important business you must handle. One of the most significant realms of endeavor at which you need to get busy making sure you succeed is living regret-free! And as we all know probably better than we'd like, an integral way to ensure that happens is by going back over relationships that have caused you regret, and healing them.

If you were a country, in other words, it would be time for you to start doing a kind of work that is among the most important any country ever does. It would be *time for you to start drawing up peace treaties with your former enemies.*

I'm serious about this. One of the most important things to do when seeking to heal a relationship that's been seriously damaged—I would go further, and say it's the most important thing—is communicate with the other person. This is exceedingly tricky and delicate when that person feels you probably don't have their very best intentions at heart, or when they have reasons of their own (no matter the degree of objective validity) to believe that in the past you have either tried to hurt them or refused to take proper responsibility for having hurt them.

You know how it is when you try to have a real conversation with someone you're not getting along with. You go into it confident that when it's over there will be nothing but love and goodwill between you, then four minutes into whatever you have to say, your entire plan for loving, productive conversation has been blown to smithereens. They didn't quite hear you right. You didn't quite say exactly what you meant. You meant to say you were only doing what you thought was right and proper and respectful—but somehow what the other person *heard* was that you think you did nothing wrong and what did go wrong between the two of you was their fault.

Don't you hate it when that happens?

Well, one of the best ways to make sure it doesn't is to write down what you want to say to the other person, and—along with a copy of your personal mission statement—give it to them. Make sure it's at least 99 percent apology and maybe 1 percent explanation or defense. (In your writing, remember how important it is to give to others as God has given to you.) Make sure it's informed by love, love—and then just a little bit more love.

Let them digest that letter in private. Let them mull it over. Let them think about what you have to say without having to simultaneously be distracted and diverted by some of the intensity that naturally attends face-to-face discussion. The great thing about a letter is that the person can return to it at different times in different moods. That way, the whole truth of it can gradually seep into them as they read and reflect.

What's important about including a mission statement along with what does (or should) amount to at least the firm beginning of a peace treaty is that later, when you see that person, you can say how seriously you take your mission statement. You can tell them it represents what it should: your highest ideals, loftiest goals, most noble ambitions. And that will be a very helpful thing to share, because part of this sharing can and should be you asking them to help hold you accountable for the values you've delineated in your statement.

A sincere letter of love and apology, along with a mission statement in which you express values that you then humbly request the other person to help you maintain? That, dear friends, is how strong, permanent alliances are made—and how lasting peace is established.

Swords Into Plowshares

> *The Lord will mediate between nations*
> *and will settle international disputes.*
> *They will hammer their swords into plowshares*
> *and their spears into pruning hooks.*
> *Nation will no longer fight against nation,*
> *nor train for war anymore.* (Isaiah 2:4)

I'm not exactly holding my breath for it to happen, but wouldn't you be thrilled to pieces if right now every single country in the world decided to adopt the above verse as its mission statement? Wouldn't you love to live in that world?

Well, until that happens, we'll just have to go on holding Isaiah 2:4 in our hearts. And it's an especially crucial sentiment to have when you're going about the blessed business of putting back together a relationship that has previously been broken apart.

Above we talked about how important it is that you move toward establishing a real peace with someone whose relationship with you has had reason to bring you regret. Initiating that process ought to start out being an exercise in fulfilling Christ's directive to us to love our enemies. But as all of us who try to do God's work on earth know, once you've begun that sort of work, you very soon find out that if anyone is benefiting from the transaction grace has moved you toward, it's you.

Jesus wasn't called the Prince of Peace for nothing. Peace is his purpose; his goal. We align ourselves with Christ when we also seek peace with others. And just as we will one day gain our reward in heaven for the sacrifice Christ made for us here on earth, so can we now, here on earth, be rewarded for doing Christ's work while we can.

When it comes to healing our broken relationships, we find we are rewarded because it's in ground that had been dug up where we can most fruitfully plant new seeds. A relationship that goes bad feels like ground that's been thoroughly plowed, doesn't it? Everything is turned up, chewed up, exposed.

And that's the land from which the very best crops always grow.

No plow, no chow, as . . . well, no one ever says that. But that doesn't mean it's not true!

Have you ever reconciled with an enemy and then found yourself almost overwhelmed with affection for that former enemy?

I'm sure you have; I think most of us have. That sentiment—that initial flush of love you feel for an erstwhile antagonist who drops his weapons and fully embraces you with his or her love—is your fertile ground. It's what you use to begin the process by which you turn a battlefield into a field rich with sustenance. However, it's not enough to simply feel that feeling; you have to use it to build upon it. Emotions flee, and you don't want this fleeing anywhere. This one, you want to keep and use.

And you want to use the joy of first peace with a former enemy as all our best and highest emotions should be used, which is to glorify God. In this context, I mean you shouldn't be shy about telling the other person about the precious emotions you are feeling for them after your reconciliation (it's almost a guarantee they're also feeling them for you). This is a tangible way God physically comes into our lives, hearts, and emotions. If the other person is a Christian, you won't have any difficulty in attributing to God the joy and delight the two of you are sharing.

If they're not a Christian, it might at first feel awkward for you to bring God so squarely into the middle of your private, magical moment. But if they've read your mission statement, they know that you believe in God. If you're reconciling with a non-Christian, be sure to communicate that you're not trying to get them to believe in Jesus—only that you think so much of what's happened between the two of you that you absolutely associate it with the highest order of love known to you.

And tell them that, just as you don't feel you have a choice but to hold in highest esteem the love Jesus so magnificently displayed during his time on earth, so you hold in esteem the love between the two of you that you so strongly feel is born of Christ.

It's important to put Christ squarely in the middle of your private, magical moment. Let them understand that as far as you're concerned, dishonoring or in any way compromising what's happened would be, to you, like dishonoring or compromising God.

What you want him or her to know is that you take making and keeping peace seriously. Well, that should do it. That should be what finally turns your swords into plowshares.

Staying the Course

We've talked about this, but it certainly bears reemphasizing. *Making peace with someone is not a goal. It's a journey.* That's why we spent the last few sections talking about how clearly you must establish who you are through your mission statement, how you should use it as an integral part of your peaceful overtures, and finally how you should take care to make sure the other person understands that you see your reconciliation as an extension of God's love for you both.

And all of that is necessary to do just so that you can begin the journey that a sustained, productive peace entails.

Must be quite the trip, huh? You don't pack like that for just any old walk through the park.

Trying to make and keep peace with someone you might not even like much is the kind of peace that makes Jesus proud to call you his brother. It's also one of the most challenging things any of us can ever do. It's an endeavor that inspires us to remember that Jesus became fully man. It's now, in your world today, in your life as you're leading it, that you're to put into practice the values that, if left as nothing but lofty ideas, wouldn't amount to anything real or significant.

Talk with the other person as often as you must in order to keep any negativity from developing between you. *Be with* them, *encourage* them, and *participate* in their lives to whatever degree is helpful and appropriate. You have to *love* them. If you don't, the whole thing will fall apart. Short of your love, the relationship is sure to unravel.

You need to love your boss who seems to the entire world as unlovable as the Abominable Snowman. You have to love your brother-in-law, even though for the life of him you just can't—with your human eyes—see what your sister sees in him. You are to love the neighbor who keeps getting your stuff wet when he waters his lawn and who loudly drags his trash cans out to the curb two hours before sunrise. You must love that colleague who keeps telling awful jokes and can't seem to fathom any humor that doesn't involve viciously making fun of others.

If you're stuck with someone, or if you've got someone in your past who's still around but with whom you never speak because of regret that transpired between you, you are to love that person as surely as God loves all his sinful followers. Anything less than love is certain to fail. Anything less, sooner or later, will run out of gas, falter, choke, stop.

Love is the only fuel that can keep a difficult relationship running smoothly and regret-free.

And that means love for the long haul.

■   ■   ■

As inspiring as the story of Jesus' journey to the cross is, I sometimes also draw a great deal of strength from the awesome travel and effort put forth by the evangelizing apostle Paul.

Sometimes I'm with a fellow ministry leader for whom I'm struggling to feel patience (much less love), or talking to someone I know I must love but just then feel more like taking him out for a drive and coming home alone. And . . . I'll remember the passage below from Galatians. And then my smile will resume its natural strength, and my heart rate will slow, and I'll actually find myself feeling grateful that person is in my life, so that I can, because of them, remember it's all about God.

> *Even before I was born, God chose me and called me by his marvelous grace. Then it pleased him to reveal his Son to me so that I would proclaim the Good News about Jesus to the Gentiles.*
>
> *When this happened, I did not rush out to consult with any human being. Nor did I go up to Jerusalem to consult with those who were apostles before I was. Instead, I went away into Arabia, and later I returned to the city of Damascus.*
>
> *Then three years later I went to Jerusalem to get to know Peter, and I stayed with him for fifteen days. The only other apostle I met at that time was James, the Lord's brother. I declare before God that what I am writing to you is not a lie.*
>
> *After that visit I went north into the provinces of Syria and Cilicia. And still the Christians in the churches in Judea didn't know me personally. All they knew was that people were saying, "The one who used to persecute us is now preaching the very faith he tried to destroy!" And they praised God because of me.*
> (Galatians 1:15–24)

The Peaceful Veteran

I titled this section "The Peaceful Veteran" because whenever I think about what a life looks like that's filled with peaceful, loving, stress-free relationships and as little regret as I've ever known anyone to carry, I think of Cap'n Mark.

Mark is a retired officer from a large metropolitan police force. He joined when he was twenty-three, and about thirty-five years later he left as one of the most respected captains ever to serve and protect the citizens of his city.

I got to know Mark years ago when he volunteered with others who were hosting an Every Man's Battle Workshop; this is a relationship I've cherished ever since.

You would think even a lifelong dedicated Christian who spent that long chasing down drug dealers, busting crime bosses, running after thieves, and wading into gang meetings would have *some* regrets. But:

> I can't say I really have any regrets. The only regrets I feel I'm vulnerable to are the ones that would come from my family. It isn't the easiest thing on a family. A cop works long hours, and, quite frankly, when you leave the house in the morning or late in the afternoon, your wife and kids don't really know if they're going to see you again. They hope they will, of course— and I sure hoped my wife and kids would see me at the end of every shift—but basically a cop's life is a bit of a crapshoot. You do your best to protect yourself and your partners, and there's a whole bunch of safety stuff you can do, but things get pretty wild out there sometimes, and sometimes they just don't go down like you expected or hoped they would.
>
> What I always made sure to do was keep my wife and my two sons up on everything that was happening with me. If something scary happened on the job that night, I wouldn't hide it from them. A lot of cops do that; they think their family, and other people they love, just can't understand what it is they go through every night when they're out there driving around, answering calls for all kinds of crimes. And in a way they're right. Their family can't really understand what it's like to be out there on the streets, armed and primed for action. But I never let that stop me from talking to my kids and wife about

my day at work. I knew that if I ended that communication, my whole family life would start to unravel.

Mark's a big, tough-looking guy, so it was a little odd hearing him talk with such ease about matters of emotional import to him. I sure encouraged him to continue telling me about his regret-free life, though.

I would say the most important thing I ever did with my family was pray. I prayed with them every morning before I left for work, and every night with them when I got home. If I was working the swing shift, I prayed with them before I left for work, and at night I would pray alone by the side of their beds when they slept. Praying with my family was the thing, I know, that kept my family strong and together during all my years on the force.

In an equally direct way, the Lord guided my actions while I was out working. I know the reason I don't have many if any regrets today is that I always worked with the Lord in mind. I let the Holy Spirit guide me in every situation. I never went anywhere without packing the Lord with me, you know? So that means I never let myself do anything I would later be ashamed of or embarrassed of. I made sure no matter who I was dealing with—pimp, dealer, snitch, gang leader, wife-beater, anybody—I treated them how I knew the Lord wanted me to. That's not to say I was always some kind of super-sweet guy or anything like that. I mean, sometimes I felt like the Lord wanted me to make sure somebody didn't get up, you know, or make sure somebody never got one of their arms loose, since I knew if they did someone was gonna get hurt. So it wasn't like I didn't do my job. But I did it, always, with God in mind. And that's why I don't have regrets today.

What a beautiful testimony! Here's a man who, God knows, has as much reason as any to live a regret-filled life, and yet his soul is just as free and open as it could be.

That's how all of us should be, at work and at home: *God-centered.*

If it worked for Mark, with the kind of life he was leading, don't you think it can work for you too? I know it can. You just have to let it.

CHAPTER 10

Accepting and Granting Forgiveness

Our lives have many purposes; there are myriad ways by which each of us measures quality of life. But Christians are motivated by a very singular and almost spectacularly overriding imperative: to follow Jesus as closely as it is within us to do.

We all want to be like Jesus. We want to listen to his counsel, read God's Word, heed his call for our lives. We want, when we pass from this life to the next, to be found worthy to remain as near to God as he has promised us we will be if we but surrender our lives to him.

We want to be the best Christians we can be. In that lies all.

What's interesting about the desire to walk as closely as possible to God is how deeply it's rooted in what to a large degree are abstract concepts. That's not to say that we can't at every moment discern God's will in our lives. By immersing ourselves in the life of a devoted follower, and by keeping our attention not on the world's material things but instead on the guiding light of the Spirit within us, we can, in fact, walk every step of our lives with God.

But in the final analysis we have to admit that God himself must remain for us largely abstract. He is so vast, so limitless, so infinitely powerful, so incomprehensibly profound, that in the end we're incapable of doing more than falling to our knees in humble wonderment.

So the question then becomes, how do we know when we've successfully followed Christ? By what signs can we be assured that we have achieved the kind of relationship with Christ to which we aspire?

In what way is the abstractness of God finally and fully translated into the concrete, tangible reality of our lives?

The answer is simple enough. *Our faithfulness to Christ is clearly and unmistakably demonstrated by the degree to which we have accepted and granted forgiveness.*

That's it. That's how you know how close you are to God. If you harbor resentments, nurture grudges, and keep track of offenses, you are away from God. If you forgive others, you are truly God's person. It's that easy.

As Paul tells us, a key feature of love is that it "keeps no record of being wronged" (1 Corinthians 13:5). And,

If you forgive those who sin against you, your heavenly Father will forgive you. But if you refuse to forgive others, your Father will not forgive your sins. (Matthew 6:14–15)

It really is all about forgiveness. We must forgive others as God, through the sacrifice of his Son, has promised his forgiveness to us. And there's nothing abstract about this love we're called upon to grant others. Anyone can love a person who hasn't ever caused offense. That's not the challenge. The challenge is to forgive those who have consciously and purposefully hurt us. If Christ can beseech the Father to forgive the very people who have beaten him and nailed him to a cross, then we can forgive people whatever offenses they've visited upon us.

First we accept Christ's forgiveness of us—and then we pass that forgiveness along to virtually everyone we ever meet and know. That's how we know how close we are to God.

That is the essential ingredient to living a regret-free life.

God's Role in Your Healing

God's role in your life is to heal you. It's not a sideshow of the relationship. It's not an offshoot of what happens when some other "real" thing between you and God is taking place. Relationship with God means your healing is what's happening. That's it; that's the main attraction. Healing you is what God has been waiting through all of eternity to do! It's why he sent Jesus Christ to earth.

I have known a lot of people who tried to heal themselves. I've tried to heal myself in the past. Of course, by "heal" what I usually meant at those times was "continue to make better." Sometimes in my life I've gotten what I think of as so big and strong, so powerful and mighty, that usually without even realizing it I became convinced the only person I really needed to bring me true peace, happiness, and contentment was me. I was successful. I had a transforming and robust ministry. I had a wonderful family. I had what I'd worked hard to obtain! Life was nothing but questions, and—lucky me—I just happened to have all the answers.

And then, as happens with people with blind spots in their lives, those blind spots become the driving force. I learned one of the hardest lessons I've ever had to learn. Not only did I not have any of the answers to life, I didn't even know the right *questions*. One minute I'm on top of the world, and the next I discover that my marriage, which had always been tough going, was over. I learned of some extremely troubling news at the same time our counselor seemed to think things were getting so much better for us. I knew that wasn't the case when I learned the ship I'd co-captained for twenty years was riddled with holes and sinking fast.

Funny, isn't it, how quickly things crumble once they begin to fall apart just a little. Not "ha-ha" funny; more like "sit down for eight hours and cry yourself into a coma" funny. But sometimes, for the big hits, it doesn't seem like things exactly take their time falling apart on you.

It's like with a sand castle. You know how, as a kid, you'd spend hours and hours building the perfect sand castle? And you'd build it just far enough away from the water so that the sand was solid enough for the walls but still wet enough to allow for those perfect, dribbled-on architectural embellishments. This separated shabby castles from yours, which was so formidable a fortress that anyone would see it could practically lead to Camelot once again being established on earth.

Remember how you used to build those kinds of sand castles?

No? Well, perhaps I was then as I am now—a tad obsessed with building things. And just like back then, I've had to learn over and over again: What man builds, God destroys.

One wave—not even a wave but one last push of a wave's water through the sand—and it's over. Everything's undermined.

And the walls come a'tumblin' down.

If your walls have come down—if you're hurting, if you're burdened with regret—that's actually good, because it means you're ready to get serious about letting God do what he most wants for your life: to heal it.

Look at this passage, just one of the many instances in which Jesus proved he is the Great Healer. If Jesus can do this for a woman's body, think what he can do for your soul!

> *One Sabbath day as Jesus was teaching in a synagogue, he saw a woman who had been crippled by an evil spirit. She had been bent double for eighteen years and was unable to stand up straight. When Jesus saw her, he called her over and said, "Dear woman, you are healed of your sickness!" Then he touched her, and instantly she could stand straight.* (Luke 13:10–13)

Verdict: You're Not Guilty

One of the main things about regret is that it's fueled by our nagging conviction that we should have done something different from whatever it is we did do. We knew then the right thing to do, but instead we chose something different. We feel we failed morally, and the knowledge that we chose to align ourselves with or enable evil is what keeps our regrets ever alive and burning within us.

But a lot of times, if you look back on what you did that's bringing you regret, you discover that, as happens so often, what seems like a matter of cut-and-dried morality is, in fact, something a whole lot fuzzier. Judges face this sort of thing all the time; it's one of the big reasons they have to go through so much training and real-life experience before they're deemed wise enough to determine the fate of the lives brought before them. A judge knows things very often aren't as clear and simple as . . . well, for one, as lawyers on either side of a typical case would like him to believe they are. They know better. They know that often there are extenuating circumstances that demand the whole matter before them be considered in a new light.

Be sure that whenever you're feeling regret about something in your past, you haven't done what people burdened by regret typically do. Don't forget about all the extenuating circumstances then at play in your life that no doubt contributed to doing whatever it is you did. Do not, in other words, remember *only* the fact of what you did. What you actually *did* doesn't exist in isolation from everything else that was going on at the moment of your transgression. There were all kinds of things happening to, with, and around you right then that contributed.

It's not that you aren't to take responsibility for whatever wrong you did. You are; taking responsibility for the wrongs you've done is crucial to your being relieved from the regret your wrong has caused you. But part of taking responsibility is also acknowledging that not everything going on at that time was your responsibility. In a way, claiming that you acted wrongly in total isolation from any extrinsic factors is sheer egoism. It puts you at the world's absolute center. It means nothing existed outside of you.

But that's just . . . well, I don't want to say stupid, but if I were to pick just one word for it, that'd be a good one. None of us ever exists in isolation from all the things going on with all people at any given moment. I might one night get drunk in a bar (not really, because I don't drink, but go with it), spark a fight, and then regret it the next morning, but that doesn't mean there was no reason for me to have been moved the night before to do such a thing.

I was probably drinking as a way to escape something awful. Maybe I'd been fired from my job. Maybe I'd just found out someone I loved very much had deceived me. Maybe I never got over how terribly my parents treated me when I was young. It's a sure thing that there was a whole host of factors that led to me going to that bar, drinking too much, and picking a fight. (Do let me say, for the record, that in addition to not drinking, I've never in my life gotten into a drunken brawl. I don't even like watching fights, much less being in them!)

When you're thinking about regrets, just remember: You're guilty *and* not guilty. Guilty for making whatever bad decision you did, not guilty for the factors that influenced you to make that bad decision.

And never forget that, in the final analysis, you don't have to feel guilty at all. None of us ever does, once we've been completely forgiven—and Jesus Christ offers full forgiveness to any and all who come to him with a truly repentant heart.

Giving as Good as You Get

You might be familiar with one or both of the passages below. But I'd still like to ask you to take a moment and read them.

The first is from Mark. In most Bibles it's placed under a heading that says "The Great Commandment"—or, as in the *New Living Translation*, "The Most Important Commandment."

> *One of the teachers of religious law was standing there listening to the debate. He realized that Jesus had answered well, so he asked, "Of all the commandments, which is the most important?"*
>
> *Jesus replied, "The most important commandment is this: 'Listen, O Israel! The Lord our God is the one and only Lord.*

And you must love the Lord your God with all your heart, all your
soul, all your mind, and all your strength.' The second is equally
important: 'Love your neighbor as yourself.' No other command-
ment is greater than these" (12:28–31).

The next passage I'd like you to read is from Matthew. (In my
Bible, it's called "Teaching About Love for Enemies.")

You have heard the law that says, "Love your neighbor" and
hate your enemy. But I say, love your enemies! Pray for those who
persecute you! In that way, you will be acting as true children of
your Father in heaven. For he gives his sunlight to both the evil
and the good, and he sends rain on the just and the unjust alike.
If you love only those who love you, what reward is there for that?
Even corrupt tax collectors do that much. If you are kind only to
your friends, how are you different from anyone else? Even pagans
do that. (5:43–47)

Now then. What else do you need to know about the importance of giving God's love as much as you get it? It's the only way
to live! It is, in fact, the very way that Jesus commanded us to
live. And it's definitely the only way to live if you want a regret-
free life.

The truth is that if you're not giving to others as much love
as you're getting from God, you're not getting as much love from
God as you should be. And that can only mean you're not allowing yourself to feel as much of God's love as you could be. It
simply cannot be the case that God doesn't love you; God *is* love
(1 John 4:8).

Our job—or, better put, our highest lot—isn't to receive love
from God. And it's not to give God's love to other people either.
Those are very good—but each is only half of what we should be

doing. The *whole* of it is simpler than either alone. What we should be doing in life—our highest purpose as humans and followers of Jesus—is to be a conduit of God's love. God's love isn't supposed to come in and stop with us. Our selves are not the end of God's love but the means. We are the way in which God's love is to be distributed throughout our little corner of the world.

It's absolutely vital that we *give* as much of God's love as we can—that we *accept* as much of God's love as we can—because that's how we achieve the ever-evasive balance we all want so badly. It is the nature of God's love to continue expressing itself outward once we've accepted it into our hearts. If we allow that to happen, we become a balanced, calm person grounded in God's love. And that is how we lay our heads upon our pillows every night, with nary a single regret to keep us awake.

The Bonding Power of Grace

I know a woman whom I'll call . . . well, Grace, since that name couldn't fit her better. Grace is one of those precious individuals who make a large church—in this case, a megachurch—function like something else. As in, if you're dealing with this church in any way that connects to her personal ministry in it, you feel less like you're at a megachurch and more like you're in one of those small, idyllic churches like perhaps one shining out from a Thomas Kinkade painting.

I believe that Grace's official job title is "Secretary." But if you're familiar with the typical church's daily life, you know that more often than not "Secretary" actually means "Person Who Runs Everything and Without Whom the Entire Church and All of Its Staff Would Collapse." Grace's efficiency, charm, work ethic, attention to detail, and ability to keep everybody focused on the big picture of any project all contribute to her being absolutely indispensable to a hundred daily little victories. Her church family is most blessed to have Grace as one of its primary matriarchs, and they all know it and love her for it.

There was a time, though, in this godly woman's life when she was confused about who she was and who God meant her to be. When she was a young woman, Grace had a baby out of wedlock and gave that baby up for adoption. Surrendering her precious little boy broke her heart, but at the time she simply couldn't see any other path to take.

Cut to twenty-eight years later. One day Grace—who had married a good man and with him had three fine children who were then in or just out of college—got a phone call from a man who, after hemming and hawing, blurted out that he was the son Grace had once abandoned.

"I was absolutely flabbergasted," Grace remembers. "I mean, nothing in your life ever prepares you for such a thing."

Like so many adopted children, Grace's natural son, Luke, had decided to take the time and trouble to find his birth mother.

"He said he wanted to meet me," says Grace. "I couldn't deny him that. And I wanted to meet him too, very much. I knew right then that God had decided to bless me with this gift of my returning son. I cried for the whole day we met, I was just so overwhelmed by it all."

When they first reunited, Grace found that she had even more reason to cry than she'd thought. She was surprised and not a little dismayed to discover that her son was a chain-smoking punk rocker.

"He was really hardcore," she recalls. "He had all these tattoos, and piercings—a couple of which were even in his face! He was dressed in rags, practically, and his hair was all crazy. He was in some band with an awful name—Death's Door or Death's Breath or something. Honestly, he looked like a heroin addict. I can tell you it was all a bit upsetting."

So what did Grace do? She prayed and prayed and prayed and prayed for God to show her a way that she could bond with Luke and even aid in the healing of his broken life.

Even though when they met, a church was probably the last place on earth Luke would ever venture, and even though the kinds of dingy clubs where Luke hung out were about the last place on earth Grace would ever willingly visit, Grace and Luke did get to know each other, in part by making a point of visiting where the other felt most comfortable.

And now, over ten years later, where do you think Grace and her son are most frequently seen together? That's right, at Grace's church.

Luke, former punk guitarist, now plays in one of his church's most popular praise brands. And he hasn't been to one of those clubs in years.

The grace of God (also being, in this case, the God of Grace) uses the transforming power of his love to bond us to those with whom he knows we're most in need of attachment. His love and divine healing of our broken hearts change us in such a way that we find ourselves able to bond with people whom we, on our own, wouldn't likely be able to.

A key to a regret-free life lies in learning to bond not just with those whom we love but also with those whom we never thought we could love. Only God can do that for us; only God can tear down the walls people construct between themselves. If you know there's someone in your life with whom you're going to regret not bonding, do what my friend Grace did. Get down on your knees, and pray to God to show you the way.

Healing Through Humility

There's a seeming dichotomy, isn't there, between (1) being healed through the power of God's transformative presence within you and (2) remaining humble. How does someone become filled with the Creator of all, the Alpha and Omega, the all-knowing, all-powerful, all-seeing cause and sustaining force of the universe—and remain humble? It almost doesn't even make sense. It's like gobbling down all the food at a Christmas feast meant for eight and then saying you're still hungry. It's just not possible. You ate more than you can hold; you can't be hungry.

You know God intimately enough to have your entire spirit and soul transformed so that you now reflect the divine love of Christ himself—yet you're humble?

How can that work? How can human knowledge of God and complete, utter humility be in the same place at the same time? Wouldn't one sort of necessarily crowd out the other?

For an answer to this quandary, and to see how continuous healing through continuous humility is possible, we need look no further than the Bible. Specifically, we can witness Paul's life. Next to Jesus, Paul is easily the most influential New Testament figure. Anything we learn from Paul we can take, literally, as gospel.

Was there ever any man more filled with the Holy Spirit than the former Saul of Tarsus? And it wasn't like the Spirit moved Paul to study, or reflect, or minister to people in a behind-the-scenes kind of way. The Spirit did move Paul to do each of those things—and do them greatly—but it also moved him to act with a forthright, courageous bravery that I think is extremely difficult for any of us today to envision.

Paul wasn't just an enthusiastic Christian; he was *the* enthusiastic Christian of his (or possibly any) time. He was so filled with God's love and energy that he was relentlessly vigorous about spreading the good word of that love out into a world that wasn't exactly thrilled to hear it. But he did it—he ceaselessly let the Holy Spirit guide and inspire him—because the Lord's power was that strong upon and within him.

How did Paul remain humble while being aware of God's having chosen him to fantastically facilitate his work on earth? In the same way you can be sure to keep yourself ever humble even as you are filled with God's power through his Spirit: by remembering your regrets.

We don't know exactly what was deep within Paul's heart and mind about his regrets. But I think a safe guess is that his having spent his pre-conversion life viciously persecuting Christians could never have been too far from his consciousness.

> *I used to believe that I ought to do everything I could to oppose the very name of Jesus the Nazarene. Indeed, I did just that in Jerusalem. Authorized by the leading priests, I caused many believers there to be sent to prison. And I cast my vote against them when they were condemned to death. Many times I had them punished in the synagogues to get them to curse Jesus. I was so violently opposed to them that I even chased them down in foreign cities.* (Acts 26:9–11)

Is there any question Paul remembered the great harm and tragedy he was personally responsible for in the lives of untold numbers? Clearly, there is not. Paul knew what he'd done. He knew the families he'd torn apart, the children from loving homes he'd left orphans, the wives he'd made destitute, the husbands he'd tortured. It's hard to imagine anyone ever having deeper regrets than the ones that surely haunted Paul.

Hopefully you don't have anything in your past as terrible as Paul did in his, but it's also a sure bet you've done things that deeply pain you to recall. And while it's important to ultimately resolve the regret you feel for those things in the ways and for the reasons we're examining, it's also true that the sheer fact you did those bad things can, like virtually everything in your life, be used by God to help you better follow God.

You know the old saying "There but for the grace of God go I"? Well, you can play both roles in that tight little drama. You *do* play both roles. No matter how close to God you are today, there have been times when you were the worst kind of sinner. *It's remembering those times at your worst that can keep you humble—even when, through the power of God, you're at your best.*

That's the one good thing about regret. You can use your memory as a way to remain humble, even while, through God's grace, you're being healed and helping to heal others.

CHAPTER 11

Resolution Through Restitution

Let's start out by defining *restitution*. Here's what I found from the *Random House Unabridged Dictionary* (© Random House, Inc., 2006):

1. reparation made by giving an equivalent or compensation for loss, damage, or injury caused; indemnification
2. the restoration of property or rights previously taken away, conveyed, or surrendered
3. restoration to the former or original state or position

You see that when I talk about resolution through restitution, I'm talking about balancing the books between you and whomever you've hurt. You need this balance if you're serious about leading a regret-free life. If you haven't done everything you can to pay back a person for whatever you took—materially or otherwise—then you'll never be able to live regret-free, because you'll always be aware of the situation that you left unresolved. And at one level or another, you'll always regret never stepping up to do the right thing.

The Bible offers us lots of guidance when it comes to restitution. For instance, "A thief who is caught must pay in full for everything he stole" (Exodus 22:3). You pay back what you owe. What could be more straightforward than that? What could be more right?

One of the most famous New Testament stories about restitution's importance is in Luke 19:2–10:

> There was a man there [in Jericho] named Zacchaeus. He was the chief tax collector in the region, and he had become very rich. He tried to get a look at Jesus, but he was too short to see over the crowd. So he ran ahead and climbed a sycamore-fig tree beside the road, for Jesus was going to pass that way.
>
> When Jesus came by, he looked up at Zacchaeus and called him by name. "Zacchaeus!" he said. "Quick, come down! I must be a guest in your home today."
>
> Zacchaeus quickly climbed down and took Jesus to his house in great excitement and joy. But the people were displeased. "He has gone to be the guest of a notorious sinner," they grumbled.
>
> Meanwhile, Zacchaeus stood before the Lord and said, "I will give half my wealth to the poor, Lord, and if I have cheated people on their taxes, I will give them back four times as much!" [referencing Exodus 22:1].
>
> Jesus responded, "Salvation has come to this home today, for this man has shown himself to be a true son of Abraham. For the Son of Man came to seek and save those who are lost."

I just love this story. It's a powerful affirmation of how we must always be ready, out of love and respect for the righteousness of Jesus Christ, who more than paid back the cost of our sins, to repay the cost of our sinning to those whom it hurt. We can't live a regret-free life, and we can't claim to be a true follower of Jesus, until we do exactly that.

Being Resolved to Solve

In a way, a relationship that isn't going right is like a puzzle you want to solve. Is it your fault that things have gone poorly between you and the other person? Was there something you should have said that you didn't, something you should have done that you didn't?

Or maybe the problem lies with the other person. *That's* a whole lot easier for you to see! The role you played in moving what should have been a healthy relationship into one that keeps you up raging or crying at night is likely to always seem a bit of a mystery to you. But it's never any problem, is it, to see where the other person messed everything up. Their sins are blatantly obvious. Their transgressions stand out like mustard splashes on a coal pile. Their wrongs are so obvious and unacceptable that it's a miracle they haven't already come crawling to you, begging your forgiveness!

Just what is the matter with other people, anyway? Why can't they just embrace their inner loser and beg your pardon?

That's the big mystery in a relationship gone wrong.

The problem, of course, is that in a bad relationship the thoughts you're having about the other person are also theirs about you. Just as you're sure you're basically innocent of wrongdoing, so too are they certain that any judge in the land, ruling on all that's ever transpired, would determine they deserve full restitution for all the outrageous pain and suffering they've so admirably endured, and that *you* need to be taken out into the town square and soundly rebuked.

You think you're right; they're sure you're as wrong as stepping on the gas when the light's turned red.

As it almost always does in matters of the heart between two people, the truth lies somewhere in the middle.

Well, if you want to lead a regret-free life, then you need to take responsibility for figuring out where, exactly, that truth does lie. You can't repay a debt if you don't know how much you owe. *One big key to regret-free living is learning your share of the damages and then figuring out what you can do to repay your debt.*

If you were a thief, it'd be enough to figure out what you owe in accordance with the kind of straight-ahead justice mentioned in the Exodus quote above. There, you simply owe what you stole. But wounded-relationship damage is hardly quantifiable in the same way. You can't just say, "There was that time, back when we were working together, when you took the credit for what we'd both done. We worked long and hard, perfecting our joint project, which we were to present together on Wednesday. But on Tuesday, unbeknownst to me, you made an appointment with the boss and presented it all by yourself. That's wrong. You snuck behind my back and took full credit for what we should have shared. I've decided this offense means you owe me $954.36. And I won't take a check, because I don't trust you; cash only. After you pay me this restitution, I'll forget all about your transgression."

Can't do that. The other person would think you're nuts. Assuming that *you* didn't take something tangible like a pencil or a set of hubcaps that you can replace in kind—assuming the damage between you is emotional—*you* must figure out two things: (1) what part of what happened between you is clearly and undeniably your fault, and (2) what is or might be the proper restitution for whatever you did wrong.

Another question: Ever notice how close the word *regret* is to *debt?* They just sound the same, don't they? I'm no expert on language, but it's just possible those words are as related as they seem to be because the bottom line is that if you owe a debt to somebody, you feel regret if you don't pay it back.

Debt = regret. If you agree, keep reading.

Putting Love Into Action

It's one thing to know you *should* do something, but sometimes quite another to actually *do* that thing. Especially when that something entails, in any part at all, admitting or acknowledging that you're wrong. That's just not something you're probably ever in a big rush to do.

If there's one thing it's easy to procrastinate about, it's admitting you erred. If law enforcement weren't around, I'm pretty sure no one but the truly innocent would ever show up for their court hearing. Who wants to, when they know their presence will guarantee the writing down of their wrongness in the record books forever?

But how much more permanent is God's record of our mortal sins than the state's log of our civil offenses? Maybe, for a while, we could put off meeting any and all earthly judges. But is there one among us capable of avoiding a meeting with the Judge of all?

No matter how sincerely we want to make restitution for our past mistakes, no matter how earnestly we want to balance the books between us and someone we've wronged, no matter how strongly we at least imagine we want to do the right thing, we still need a little something extra to actually get us off our couches, don't we?

We have almost everything we need to make that reconciling phone call or write that confessionary letter or pay that healing visit . . . but only almost. When push comes to shove, we usually still find we're not quite able to push or shove ourselves up and get busy apologizing. We're usually still missing that certain, final, motivating *something*.

And just what is this certain, final ingredient we know we're missing if we lack that ultimate, necessary motivation? It's love. *Love is always what we need to let into our hearts if we're seeking to empower ourselves to move from whoever we are and wherever we're at to whoever and wherever we want to be.*

Strong as it might be, the desire to save your reputation probably won't be enough to get you to pay restitution to someone you've wronged. Neither will be a need to always seem like a nice person. Knowing everyone will like you if you do the right thing isn't likely to do it.

But love? It's true what they say. Love really does conquer all.

And I'll bet I don't have to tell you where to look for the inspiration to love. The one inspiration certain to prove strong enough to get even the most recalcitrant non-confessor to start wondering to whom he should apologize first. Where else but the cross?

Jesus on the cross stands forever as the greatest possible symbol of love in action. Jesus didn't just *say* he loved us. He didn't just *announce* that he wanted to do everything he could so that full restitution for our sins could be forever made. He didn't just *talk* about how happy it would make him if we could spend all of eternity with him in heaven. He didn't only *speak* of how he hoped that, while we're still on earth, we could be constantly comforted by the gift of the Holy Spirit, the fullness of God inside us.

No. *Jesus proved through his actions just how seriously he took his words.* He acted in such a way that we could forever know, in the end, that his words couldn't even begin to do justice to the full magnitude of what, out of love, he was motivated to do for us.

If we're going to assess and finally pay full restitution to those whom we have wronged so that we can begin living a life free of regret, then we must turn to the love of Jesus as a means of transforming ourselves into someone who, like him, is willing to do what it takes to bring peace and harmony to the world inside and outside ourselves.

First love God with all your heart, mind, and strength, and then love your neighbor—especially one you've wronged—as you love yourself. That's one law we should all be able to obey.

Spelling It All Out

I don't like spelling. It's too exact for me. As someone who struggles with ADD, I can tell you that having to slow down and make sure every word I type is spelled right is like looking up at the night sky and, instead of just enjoying the stars, having to correctly identify each one by name. It just takes a lot of fun out of the moment.

Thank goodness there's spell check. I can usually get a word close enough for spell check to be able to tell what I *meant* to say, and then offer me the choice of getting it perfectly right.

Don't you wish there was a "spell check" for your life? Wouldn't it be great if at the end of every day you could go out into your garage, or maybe into your closet, and hit the big "Life Check" button? And then, one by one, examine each moment of that day in which you had to make a moral decision, and if in a given moment you had erred—done something even slightly selfish, been even just a little dishonorable, shown even the tiniest bit of greed—you'd be offered other good choices?

Then you'd look at the possible decisions—to say it better, to do the more morally correct thing—and, if you wanted one, choose it.

And then, just like magic, what you *did* do would be instantly replaced by your new, better choice! You, and everyone who experienced you in that moment, wouldn't remember or be affected by what you actually did but instead by your Life Check replacement option.

Just as after spell checking you know you can with more confidence send that document out, you could, having run Life Check over your whole day, go to sleep knowing you did no harm and only good.

What a blessing!

Remember, you heard the idea of Life Check here first.

Until someone invents and patents it, though, we must arrange for our own life checking. And it's important that we do. The closest thing to a Life Check application is a trusted, wise friend or counselor willing to look at your situation and suggest those wonderful options you need to have. Alone, we have no Life Check. Connected, we actually do, when we're humble enough to ask for the help.

■ ■ ■

The devil really is in the details, and we need to make sure that when we're looking back at a relationship to see where and how exactly it got off track, we stop at every mistake indicator to see if we can't identify what exactly happened. Then, once we have our list, we must go to the other person and, carefully and fully, spell out what we believe happened at any or all of the relationship's difficult moments.

That's the thing about spell check. It only recognizes and/or suggests words that are spelled exactly right. Close enough isn't good enough—it shouldn't be good enough for you either. And you can bet that close enough sure won't be sufficient for the person to whom you're presenting your take on what went wrong. If you want him or her to really listen and respect what you have to say, your explanation of what happened will need to be straightforward and precise.

It's like with a contract. It can't have loopholes or (despite how such things usually appear to people not fluent in legalese) fuzzy language. It can't be ambiguous. There's too much at stake to leave things open to interpretation.

This principle applies when it comes to relational restitution. The key to restitution—the very definition of the word, as we saw earlier—is to pay back in full what you owe. And when it comes to emotional restitution, that means first understanding and agreeing upon exactly what happened—so that proper restitution can be measured. Who did what, to whom? Who should have done what, instead of what they did do? Who was wronged? How does it get made right?

Once you get all of that spelled out for yourself—and once you know, of course, that you've been as honest as you can be—then you can take all of it, and present it, and see what the other person makes of it.

Then, if you agree on what happened, and each of you pays the restitution to the other that the facts warrant, it'll be just like you each hit your own private Life Check button and changed your wrong choices.

Signing on the Dotted Line

As I'm sure you know, a contract is a document that defines (usually as only lawyers can begin to understand) a relationship between two parties. The idea is that both parties read the contract, agree that it stipulates everything they want (or can at least live with), and then sign their name to it as a way of showing their support for it.

When you want to make restitution to someone for a wrong you've done, you have to *commit* to that restitution. You can't waffle on it or question its validity halfway through, or change your mind and decide you'd rather let things stay as they are. As many men know, you don't just *say* to your wife something like, "I'm so sorry I forgot our anniversary. I tell ya what. I'll make it up to you by taking you out to a big dinner. We'll paint the town!" If within the next few days the husband doesn't take his wife out for a wonderful night, he's going to have far more trouble on his hands than he would have if he'd just said he'd forgotten. That would have been bad enough. But to promise to make up that lapse, and then not carry through on something important he'd pledged?

Well, I don't even want to think about what's gonna happen to that man. Let's just say that if I were him (and I never, ever have been, of course), I'd start sleeping with one eye open.

■ ■ ■

Part of the process of achieving resolution through restitution is fully and absolutely committing to defining and paying the restitution honestly due. Your commitment to its being essential that the other person be compensated (though that's too strictly monetary a word) for the wrong you did is indispensable to reaching a joint, peaceful resolution between the two of you. If in your communications you in any way indicate that you're not fully committed to resolving your relationship, two things are going to bring that resolution to a screeching halt. One of those things is you; the other is the other person.

No one ever does anything as difficult as giving emotionally to another (in the deep way that's necessary to heal a broken relationship) unless they're 100 percent committed to doing exactly that. And the other person isn't otherwise going to stick around for the process of reconciliation as you've defined it, because who wants to get all dressed up for a ball they don't feel they've been invited to? You can *say* you want to reconcile, but if you don't in very plain ways show and prove that you do, then you can't expect the other person to take it seriously. Why should they take it any more seriously than you do? You can't shake hands with someone who's not really offering you their hand. You can't play cards with someone who won't stop shuffling the deck.

There's a reason contacts are legally binding. A person's good name is one of their most precious possessions, and by voluntarily signing it to a set of conditions and definitions, they are stating in the strongest possible terms their absolute commitment to them. It means they are willingly bound by their honor to uphold the terms. That's the kind of commitment you have to make to someone with whom you're truly determined to achieve resolution through restitution. It has to be good enough, and has to mean enough to you, for you to put your name on it.

The important thing to remember when you make a "deal" to fairly and generously work out your problems is that you also simultaneously make that same promise to God. God is listening to you when you say you're going to do the right thing, when you say you're going to make him proud, when you assert that you're going to let his Spirit determine your thoughts and actions. So don't commit to something as Christlike as healing with someone else unless you're entirely serious about doing it. But once you *are* that serious—once you've decided you're going to do everything you can to heal a hurting relationship—then work out the details of your terms of reconciliation, and in your heart of hearts, with God as your witness, sign on the dotted line of your promissory note to do the right thing by the other person.

Embracing Your Role

There's one thing about putting forth the thought, prayers, time, and effort to thoroughly and honestly identify the role you've played in your past—specifically, those times when you've chosen to play the kind of movie role you'd expect to see listed as "Villain" or "Thief" or "General Creep." Once you've established who you really were and what you really did, you face a very difficult choice. *Do you reject your discovered truth* about the less-than-admirable role you played (or, more commonly, in lieu of outright rejecting it, begin to right away modify or make excuses)? *Or do you do the opposite and embrace the role?*

Do you start lying to yourself about what you really did, or do you hold to the conclusion that what the Lord has shown you is the truth?

Do you embrace what you've done to or with the person you've fallen out of a good relationship with, or do you reject it—say it didn't happen, look for excuses for what you did, start telling yourself a different story than the one you know is true?

Whether you embrace or reject the role you've played in past dysfunctions—either those that have caused you regret or those you can tell right now will—is vital. The answer will determine the quality of your future life. The truth is, *you can't embrace—you can't empower—the person you want to be in your future until you've thoroughly embraced the person you've been in your past.* No matter how awful that past person is—no matter how terribly or dishonorably he or she acted—you still have to embrace him or her so that from this experience you can derive the strength needed to assure that you never again become that person.

■　■　■

We like to think this isn't true. We like to think we can essentially turn our back on who we've been, the terrible things we've done, the meanness of spirit we've displayed, the harm we've visited upon others. We feel each day is a new one—the past is the past—and we've gotten over the bad things that have happened to us, so the people we've done bad things to should do the same. We tell ourselves this sort of thing over and over again, in the hopes that we'll finally believe it.

Well, we never have believed it, and we never will. Our true selves—our godly selves—know different. You can't lie to the Holy Spirit. You can't fake out the Spirit, even for a moment. God knows who you've been and what you've done better than you know yourself.

What God is waiting for you to embrace is who you've been. God wants you to admit the bad things you've done, the role you've played in the unraveling of what should be the tight relationships in your life.

And one of the biggest reasons is that God knows that down this path conviction, confession, and redemption await you.

If you keep telling yourself that what you've done isn't that bad, that the reason you arrived at a difficult point isn't really much (if any) of your fault, then you're saying it's more important that you have a good opinion of yourself than that you avail yourself of God's forgiving grace.

Refusing to acknowledge and embrace your sinful past is choosing your love for yourself over your love of God. It's saying, "*I'll* judge. I'll decide who I was, and am. *You* just make sure you've got a place waiting for me in heaven."

That's not going to work, and you know it.

The key to fixing broken relationships—the key to beginning your new, regret-free life today—is realizing how guilty you've been in your past. Doing that means admitting you're broken. And it's not until you admit you're broken that God can finally begin to fix you.

And once you're fixed, you can start fixing your relationships with others. That's the way it works—and that's the only way it works.

Before you can stand up straight before another person, you have to fall on your knees before God.

A Final Word on Restitution

It's easy to trap yourself into the expectation that someone owes you and needs to make restitution. Most likely they won't, though. And there you'll be, stuck—unless you forgive and move on. So while you know that restitution from someone who's hurt you would make a lot of things right in your heart, don't break your own heart by waiting for something that may never come.

Feel free to suggest restitution, of course. But don't ruin your own life because someone else chooses to walk around with the burden of an unpaid debt. Forgive them. Don't forget what they did, but forgive them completely, because when we forgive, we bless ourselves with the freedom to move on.

CHAPTER 12

Restoring
Warmth and Trust

A very good friend of mine whom I'll call Bill had the worst possible relationship with his father. They didn't argue and curse at each other. They didn't rail and harangue. They didn't argue vociferously and then retreat, hurt and insulted, back into their corners before beginning yet another round of active hostilities. They didn't stab each other in the back. They didn't spread gossip to other family members.

Their relationship was worse than any of that. At least when you're fighting with someone, you're in some way communicating. Bill and his father didn't communicate at all. They didn't talk in person. They didn't exchange letters; they didn't call; they didn't send the occasional e-mail; they didn't even use carrier pigeon or Morse code.

In their relationship, every night was silent night. Holey night—for there truly was a hole right through the middle of Bill's life.

And that hole had remained for twenty-five years. Bill had left his home when he was still a teenager. He'd talked to his father once or twice more, and that was it. Bill grew into a young man, got married, had three children, excelled at two different careers, started a third . . . and through it all, he'd never had a word with his father. His wife had never met her father-in-law. His little boy and two daughters wouldn't have known their own grandfather from any other man on the street.

Then one day, with the help and guidance of dear friends who prayed for and with Bill until—praise the Lord!—the Holy Spirit was awakened within him, Bill came to Jesus. He was about thirty-eight when he finally fell into the arms of his heavenly Father, who from Bill's birth had never for a moment stopped trying to communicate with him.

Bill hadn't been filled with the love of Jesus for long at all before he was moved by the Spirit to reconcile his relationship with his father.

> I never thought I had regrets about the way I had treated my father. To me, I had always simply responded in exact accord with the things he had said and done to me. Plus, I was so young when I said some of the harsh things to him that I did, that I forgave myself for that reason too. But once I came to the Lord, I realized (1) I wasn't all that young when I said and did some of the hurtful things—I knew what I was doing; and (2) If God, through the power of his son, Jesus Christ, could forgive me and show me the love he had, why shouldn't I forgive my father? How could I feel and show any less love and forgiveness for my earthly father than my heavenly Father had so clearly shown for me? Suddenly, I realized, the rules had changed.

And did they ever. Today, some ten years after Bill's conversion, Bill and his father are as close as father and son can be.

For this chapter I'll use the story of their restoration as a source of learning and inspiration for how we, helped with the Lord's forgiving love, can restore warmth and trust to any relationship desperately in need.

Every Fire Starts With Kindling

When Bill, via the guiding light of God's holy grace, began to see that he should get back in touch with his father and try his best to heal a long-broken relationship, do you know what the first thing Bill did was?

He waited.

Have you ever heard of *kairos* and *chronos,* two ancient Greek words used to denote time? The latter is the source from which we derive words like *chronicle* and *chronology.* Chronos refers to literal, quantitative time. It's time that we can—and to some extent should—control. (If we don't control chronos, look what happens to it: The mythological god Chronos, who was nothing if not uncontrolled, ate his children! Those Greeks knew a thing or two about the importance of time management.) Chronos is time in its measurable, objective, predictable sense.

Kairos, as a concept of time, is radically different. Kairos refers to the immeasurable, subjective, and unpredictable; it's time that's not bound to any kind of quantitative category. Kairos is qualitative time; in effect, kairos goes into, not across. *Kairos time is always in the now, and so it remains an unbroken whole.*

When Jesus announced, "The time promised by God has come at last!" and "The Kingdom of God is near! Repent of your sins and believe the Good News!" (Mark 1:15), the word for "time" is *kairos*.

Again, when Paul writes, "The time that remains is very short" (1 Corinthians 7:29), the word he uses is *kairos*.

Put simply, chronos is human time, while kairos is God's. And they're not the same kind of "time" at all.

When we are with God—truly imbued with his Spirit, having given over our human will to the divine will of he who animates us all—we are on kairos time. You know how it is when you're filled with the Spirit. You seem to be in regular life but at the same time just outside or beyond it. It feels in a way as if you're floating above the world, even while you feel as grounded in the world as ever.

But one of the things you're especially aware of when filled with the Spirit is how basically *weird* your relationship with time becomes. When you are seeing and experiencing the world through God's eyes, a minute can feel like an hour, an hour like a minute. You don't really know. And (hallelujah!), you don't really care.

You don't care to look at your watch because you're on the ultimate in vacation time. You're on kairos time.

Well, Bill was very definitely on extended kairos time following his conversion. I knew Bill at that chronological time, and for months (and still, really!) he had that almost dazed, euphoric gleam in his eye characteristic of those who are firmly kairos-rooted.

He knew, soon after being saved, that he was going to reconcile with his father. He was awakened to the regrets he'd been carrying around in his heart all those years about what he had done to contribute to the broken state of the relationship, and he knew his father had to be burdened with his own regrets about what had happened between them.

But Bill didn't rush into doing anything. *He waited.*

He was on kairos time, and so he knew—he intuited—that God would tell him what to do next.

Pray Tell

It's an extremely common phrase (though not as common as it once was), but one of my favorite word combinations is the little gem "Pray tell." I love how it puts so closely together two words that are at once so distant and yet, when placed in this order, seem so perfectly related.

Pray tell. Covers just about everything, doesn't it?

Pray—and then tell!

When Bill felt the Holy Spirit urging him to be reconciled with his earthly father as he had been reconciled with his heavenly Father, he prayed. He prayed for guidance. He prayed for understanding. He brought to the Lord his understanding of the history between him and his father and asked him what to do. Then he waited as patiently as a saint for the answer to come to him in God's (kairos) time.

■ ■ ■

This was a beautiful way to respond to the presence and calling of the Holy Spirit. How often do we just assume that we know the right thing to do, then run off and do it—even though we may be running off in an entirely wrong direction because we didn't wait to hear God's whole answer to our problem? How often do we basically nod to God as we rush out the front door toward our current challenge without ever really taking the time and having the patience to listen to the entirety of his response?

Bill didn't do that. Bill waited.

Bill got his answer. And when he did, Bill sat down at his computer and started a letter that began with "Dear Dad."

Bill's letter told all about his conversion experience, how it had left him feeling like he very much wanted to get back in touch. He knew what strong anti-religion sentiments his father maintained, but he also knew he needed and wanted to be entirely honest about everything, including everything he (now) thought and felt about his father.

Bill knew that after a twenty-five-year silence this might all be a bit much to cram into one letter, so—again, responding to God's kairos time—Bill didn't make the letter too long or too dense. He told his dad about his wife, his children, his work, and his salvation.

Mostly, he told his dad how much he loved him.

And then, after having put into the envelope a picture of his kids and wife, he mailed the letter to his father (whose mailing address he had gotten from one of his brothers).

I love this episode in their reconciliation story, because Bill's behavior and response to the Spirit stands as a perfect model of what we should do when we too are moved to reconcile with others so that we can move on to living regret-free. Bill wrote a letter in which he declared his love to a father who hadn't shown him a lick of love in two decades. Bill asked nothing in return. He didn't demand, didn't accuse, and didn't bring up anything old and potentially troubling.

He simply declared his love. He told his father he loved him.

Pray tell. Bill prayed, and he told. And thus did he put into play what we all must if we want to heal with anyone in our lives: God's enduring, patient, grace-filled love.

Letting Time Work Its Magic

After Bill sent that first letter, he waited without really "waiting" at all. That is, he waited in chronos (man's) time—in measurable, clock-and-calendar time—but since he was in kairos (God's) time, he already had everything he could ever want emotionally.

And that worked for him, because he didn't get a response.

Maybe a week or so after sending that first letter, he felt moved by the Spirit to sit down and write his father a second, essentially a simple continuation of the first. In his first letter Bill had talked about the kinds of people his wife and children were; about how his daughter always had a real thing for music, about how one of his sons had always displayed a keen interest in the physical structure of things; about how his wife had a work ethic that made his seem just right for a three-toed sloth.

Now Bill wrote more about the trajectory of his wife's professional career; about how his daughter had become a professional cellist; about how the son who'd always been so drawn to investigating structures was now a junior partner at a prestigious architectural firm. Whereas in the first letter he'd told of how his youngest son had always seemed to care so much for other children, in this letter he went a bit deeper into how it was that his son had come to be the executive director of a nonprofit organization that fed hundreds of homeless people a day.

It was really just another letter one might write to anyone with whom they were trying to catch up. But in the final section, Bill wrote again of his love for his father. In Bill's words once more,

> I didn't really say much. I just told him that in all the years that had passed between us, I missed not having him in my life. I told him how often I'd envied others my age when I saw what good relationships they had with their fathers—or

any relationship at all. I told him I loved him and had no interest in arguing with him over any of the things we used to argue so much about. I told him all that sort of thinking was dead to me now, that I wanted to once again have him in my life.

Two more weeks went by without a response at all from his father.

I didn't really care, because I'd said what I wanted to say. I didn't want him to do anything that made him uncomfortable. If he preferred to remain out of touch with me, that was fine. It wouldn't have been my first choice, of course, but what could I do? I had to give him time. He's a free man. Like any of us, he's only going to do what he feels comfortable with.

Two weeks after the second letter, Bill wrote his father a third. This time, instead of simply saying that he loved him, Bill told his father exactly why he loved him. He spoke of all the things that he loved and admired. How he'd always worked so hard. How he never once spanked him or his brothers. How he didn't drink or swear or do any of the things so many of his friends' fathers routinely did. How he'd always been there for the family. Part of his third letter read:

You were an excellent role model for me. Now that I have kids of my own, I've seen how readily I used to take for granted all the qualities in you that were, in fact, special, powerful, purposeful, and truly invaluable. I don't think a day goes by in my life when something doesn't happen that makes me think gratefully of you, and your impact on my life.

In the following weeks, Bill wrote two more letters to his father.

About five months after Bill had begun writing, he went out to his mailbox, and there, lo and behold, was a letter from his father, inviting Bill and his wife out to the home in which, for the past fifteen years, he'd resided with his wife, Bill's stepmother.

■ ■ ■

Bill had let the sheer magic of time work its wonders. He let God, in God's time, do what God needed to do. It's a lesson for us all. What we rush—what we insist we do on our schedule, according to our emotional needs—can't be, in the end, anywhere near as effective as what will happen if we open up our hearts to God and do whatever he says, however he says, whenever he says.

If you're seeking to heal an important relationship that's broken, remember: "We know that God causes everything to work together for the good of those who love God and are called according to his purpose for them" (Romans 8:28).

Knowing When to Back Off

When Bill began the process of reconciling with his father—that is, of beginning to deal with the relationships of his past that had left him with regrets he finally wanted to shed—he knew, right away, one thing: It was going to be a process. It wasn't going to happen overnight. His father wasn't going to show up one fine afternoon, ring his doorbell, throw open his arms when Bill answered the door, and cry out, "My son! I've returned! I love you! I want you back in my life!"

Bill knew, going in, that getting back together with his father was going to take a lot of chronos.

What Bill also knew was that, like any long journey, the one back to peace with his father was going to have ups and downs. The road back to peace with someone you've long since broken with—especially anyone as important as a direct family member—will have its dips, bumps, turns, and long, easy stretches.

What Bill had to do was never stop listening to God. He knew that if he let God pace him, let God direct his words and actions, let God tell him when to move close and when to back off, then in the end everything would work out.

Bill and his wife, Judy, did go visit Bill's father and stepmother, and it was a wonderful experience for Bill.

> It was really kind of odd, how normal it was. I mean, here I hadn't seen my father since I was a teenager, and yet it was really like no time at all had passed. It was weird to see how differently my dad had changed physically. In my head, of course, he'd remained as young as he was when I'd last seen him. Same thing with my stepmother; it was hard not to just keep staring at her, since the last time I'd seen her, she'd been in the prime of her beauty. I'm sure they felt the same way about me. Their young, muscular teenage boy had become a somewhat flabby, balding, middle-aged man. I definitely caught them each staring at me a couple of times.

One of the reasons Bill and his father had suffered such a falling out had to do with Bill's stepmother, whom Bill's dad had married when Bill was about fourteen. Put simply, they had not gotten along, as in the way two spiders in a jar do not get along—which is to say, at all.

On their initial visit, Bill and Judy stayed fourteen days.

That was too long. It was a great time, and I wouldn't take a minute of it back. But at the end of the two weeks, it was time to go, you know? The cracks were starting to show. My stepmother did an admirable job of hiding it, but you could tell toward the end there that our mere presence was beginning to wear on her just a little bit. And who could blame her? The two of them had barely had anyone else in their house at all in years, and here we were, dragging all our crackling history in with us, hanging around for two weeks!

So when they returned home, Bill called his father and stepmother, thanked them very much for the wonderful time they'd shown him and his wife, and then didn't contact them again for three or four weeks.

It was time to back off. Bill, who had the long haul in view, said, "It's like with rice. If you keep taking the lid off the pot and stirring the rice around, you're guaranteed to ruin it. Sometimes you just have to let things sit."

When you're trying to bring the warmth and trust back into a broken relationship, consider the wisdom Bill so lovingly put into action:

> *For everything there is a season,*
> *a time for every activity under heaven.*
> *A time to be born and a time to die.*
> *A time to plant and a time to harvest.*
> *A time to kill and a time to heal.*
> *A time to tear down and a time to build up.*
> *A time to cry and a time to laugh.*
> *A time to grieve and a time to dance.*
> *A time to scatter stones and a time to gather stones.*
> *A time to embrace and a time to turn away.*

A time to search and a time to quit searching.
A time to keep and a time to throw away.
A time to tear and a time to mend.
A time to be quiet and a time to speak.
A time to love and a time to hate.
A time for war and a time for peace. (Ecclesiastes 3:1–8)

Giving Before You've Gotten

There are a lot of things I like about Bill's amazing story. One of my favorite elements is how, throughout it all, he so utterly exemplified one of the most important gospel lessons: *Give before you get.*

It's so simple, isn't it? Don't wait to give until you receive; anyone can give something after they've first been given something themselves. Giving under any situation or condition is good, of course; giving as Bill did to his father, though, before you get anything at all, is one of the surest signs you're listening to and obeying God's direct will for your life. It's the sure way to wind up living regret-free.

Nowhere is this directive more clearly illustrated than in the parable of the lost son. This is one of the most well-known biblical stories specifically because its message is so simple. If you haven't read it before, please do; here, let's cut to the part of the story that teaches the lesson about giving first and asking questions later (if ever).

So [the prodigal son] returned home to his father. And while he was still a long way off, his father saw him coming. Filled with love and compassion, he ran to his son, embraced him, and kissed him. His son said to him, "Father, I have sinned against both heaven and you, and I am no longer worthy of being called your son."

But his father said to the servants, "Quick! Bring the finest robe in the house and put it on him. Get a ring for his finger and sandals for his feet. And kill the calf we have been fattening. We must celebrate with a feast, for this son of mine was dead and has now returned to life. He was lost, but now he is found." So the party began.

Meanwhile, the older son was in the fields working. When he returned home, he heard music and dancing in the house, and he asked one of the servants what was going on. "Your brother is back," he was told, "and your father has killed the fattened calf. We are celebrating because of his safe return."

The older brother was angry and wouldn't go in. His father came out and begged him, but he replied, "All these years I've slaved for you and never once refused to do a single thing you told me to. And in all that time you never gave me even one young goat for a feast with my friends. Yet when this son of yours comes back after squandering your money on prostitutes, you celebrate by killing the fattened calf!"

His father said to him, "Look, dear son, you have always stayed by me, and everything I have is yours. We had to celebrate this happy day. For your brother was dead and has come back to life! He was lost, but now he is found!" (Luke 15:20–32)

I often wonder about the older son. I wonder if he got the message of his father's instinctive, God-filled, automatic, unquestioning display of love for his brother. We can all understand his frustration; he's been striving every day, being an honorable son to an honorable father—and here his dissolute little brother comes traipsing in from nowhere and gets treated like a favored prince!

It's always my hope that the brother is won over by his father's way of giving to those he loves before he even thinks of the cost to himself. That's what real love is. It takes no account of payments due but keeps paying and paying and paying. It never runs out. God—*love*—is a well that simply cannot run dry.

If there's a relationship in your life to which you're trying to restore warmth and forgiveness, remember the father of the prodigal son. Without ignoring or readily dismissing the objections of the older boy—that is, without acknowledging that you yourself have no doubt been hurt by the other person—focus most on what the father, despite what it's easy to think of as "fair" or "right," did anyway. Remember how he fully gave out of love, not measuring his giving or what he'd lost.

Then go forth to do the same with those who have been lost to you.

CHAPTER 13

Loving and Giving Out of Fullness

One of the most interesting people I've ever met was a man I'll call Dan, a successful marketing executive in the advertising business. If I showed you a gigantic poster with every brand image on it that he in some way has been responsible for, you'd begin to have some idea of his impact on worldwide culture.

I met Dan when he attended a New Life weekend. He and his wife, "Sue," had reached a patch in their twenty-year marriage where they both felt something like our weekend might do them some good.

It did. When we finished, Dan came to thank me for the wonderful breakthroughs both he and Sue had experienced. I was glad he came forward, because I had taken special note of him throughout the weekend. Something about him had just struck me as interesting, so I was glad for the chance to get to know him even a moment or two longer than our time together had already afforded.

We subsequently developed a friendship. The more I got to know Dan, the more I realized that at least half (if not all) of the problems that continued to make his personal life less than his smashing professional success could be attributed to his having treated his personal life in the same way he treated his professional life.

This isn't really that atypical. Many people, especially men—so many of whom have, after all, been raised to believe that their primary function in life is to succeed in business—practice interpersonal communication the same way at home as at work. Sometimes that's good; sometimes it's not. The problem with it for Dan was that he, in a very real sense, was a professional pitchman; he made a living telling people what he already knew they most wanted to hear.

In fact, he made a great living doing this, because those whose dreams he was helping to make reality were people with nearly unlimited wealth who ran companies that produced products or services to millions with already-proven loyalty. Dan basically was a spell weaver, a charmer.

The problem was that Dan's sons didn't much respect him. His only daughter told him she had long ago given up communicating with him. His wife wished he would "open up" more with her.

And as I got to know Dan better, I realized he was telling his family and friends what he thought they wanted to hear. Dan is a good guy; he wants to please people, and his communication style was how he'd learned to accomplish it. But at heart, in his communications with loved ones, he was insincere. And not only can people sense that—inevitably, they recoil from it.

As Dan is continuing to learn every day, you can't give to people you love anything but the real you. Not what you think they want, not what you think will make them feel good about you or themselves or life or anything else. Just you. Raw, broken, honest, unplugged you.

If you're not giving from your heart, don't give at all.

And what should be in your heart? God.

The only way to love and give is to do both out of the fullness of God. Nothing else ever works anyway.

So let's spend a little time looking at how to love and give out of the Spirit's benevolent fullness. We don't ever want to create a reason for those nearest to us, or ourselves, to feel regret.

Keeping Your Well Filled

As we've seen all along, one of the most important things to bear in mind about healing a broken relationship is that it doesn't happen overnight. It'd be nice if you could do it with nothing but the right Hallmark card and some beautiful flowers, but it doesn't work that way. We must bring more to the table.

Fixing a broken relationship is a long process. Sometimes it can take months or even years. And because bringing together two people who have moved far apart takes tremendous time and effort, one must prepare accordingly. You wouldn't take off hiking in the woods for two weeks with nothing but what you could fit in your pants pockets. You'd starve to death. Instead, you'd pack everything needed for going the long haul.

You get ready for your big trip, and once you're prepared as can be, you start off by pacing yourself. You don't start running. You don't skip. You don't scamper on the trail for two hundred feet, and then stop—and then start running again. You'd be exhausted before the first mile.

What you do is walk at an easy, comfortable pace. You walk understanding that you have a very long way to go, and that the only way to get there in one piece is to take it easy, listen to your body, and move along at a rate that will ensure you don't burn out from going too fast or get stalled in making any progress at all.

Same with a relationship you're trying to heal. Take it slowly, and take it steadily. You have to think about what you're doing. You can't plan ahead with the same kind of exactness as when planning a hiking or camping trip, but you can certainly bear in mind that, just like with an excursion outdoors, healing a relationship will entail all kinds of steps, periodic assessments of progress, and fruitful planning ahead.

It won't, in other words, be effortless.

The thing about a long hiking trip is that you have to remember to bring along *all kinds of things*. I love to go backpacking, but sometimes, when I've laid out on the floor everything I'm going to carry, I only want to lie down and take a nap, because I can't begin to imagine hoisting all that stuff up on my poor bent back. But when it comes to creating a loving, healthy bond out of what may now be only a source of stress and regret, there's only *one thing* you must have with you the whole time.

And, like water on a hiking trip, it has to be the one thing you know for sure will never deplete: *the fullness of God in your heart.*

Fixing a broken relationship is all about loving and giving from a heart filled with God's compassionate presence. A heart filled with the joyous appreciation of all that God can make of us. It needs nothing. It asks for nothing. It just wants to give and give and give until the object of its giving is at a loss to do anything but, finally, accept that love.

That is how you heal a broken relationship. You give out of the fullness of your heart, which refills itself, right up to the top, in exact equal measure to whatever of its love is joyfully given to another.

The key, of course, is to learn how to never run out of the fullness of God's love.

Turning to the Source

After Jesus left the synagogue with James and John, they went to Simon and Andrew's home. Now Simon's mother-in-law was sick in bed with a high fever. They told Jesus about her right away. So he went to her bedside, took her by the hand, and helped her sit up. Then the fever left her, and she prepared a meal for them.

That evening after sunset, many sick and demon-possessed people were brought to Jesus. The whole town gathered at the door to watch. So Jesus healed many people who were sick with various diseases, and he cast out many demons. But because the demons knew who he was, he did not allow them to speak.

Before daybreak the next morning, Jesus got up and went out to an isolated place to pray. (Mark 1:29–35)

There is nothing I or anyone else can say that more perfectly captures how vital it is that every one of Jesus' followers takes time out every day to go to their own "isolated place" and pray to God for strength. If Jesus had to pray for spiritual strength and inspiration, how much more important is it for us mere mortals to do the same?

It amazes me how few Christians set aside time in their everyday lives to put down their concerns of the moment, sit, read Scripture, and pray to God. How much better would your life be if you took the time to do that every single day? Are you too busy running here and going there, taking care of this and handling that, to remember to care for the soul God has entrusted to you?

There are as many great reasons to regularly pray to God as there are to live and breathe and stay alive. One of the greatest is the good it can do you as you struggle to heal a broken relationship. Once again, the key to successfully healing the wounds between you and another is to give. Give your love. Give your peace. Give your generosity of spirit. Give your heart. Give, above all, your forgiveness.

The issue with that is, if you give away as much of something as you possibly can, you're going to run out. How can supply and distribution work that way? On Halloween, you don't open your door, see a cute little cowboy or ballerina with a pumpkin or sack held out expectantly, and just start dumping all your candy, do you?

(Actually, I have a bad habit of doing almost exactly that. *And* they're so cute I want to give them not only all the candy on hand but also any cookies or snacks we happen to have in our house. My wife has learned that when it comes to properly dispensing the candy, it's best to leave me out of the picture.)

If you do give out all the candy too soon, what do you have to do? Run back to the store and buy more. (And there's never any of the good stuff left, and you spend the rest of the night giving the yucky generic candy that makes kids look in their sack and then back up at you with that disappointed look no one ever likes to see from a kid.)

Well, what must all God's children do if we want to make sure we never run out of the love we keep on giving? Turn and run to God to get more. Only he can keep us in full supply of all the love we need if we're going to keep giving as much as we can. *He* can keep those sacks full. And with the good stuff too.

Once more, if Jesus felt it necessary, after all his giving and healing, to very soon thereafter turn to God in order to replenish his supply of love, compassion, and strength, do we really think we can, or should, do anything different?

Never forget, when you're doing the loving business of healing with another, to return, every single day, to the source of all our healing.

Giving Is Receiving

As I write this, a Christmas season has just passed. Like all (or most, anyway), this one was filled with all the love and generosity of spirit that marks any celebration centered on our Savior, Jesus Christ.

This year I was particularly blessed to be part of an endeavor that I think, as much as any I've ever experienced, exemplified what it really means to say it's better to give than to receive. It's so good to give; in fact, I believe that giving actually is receiving.

One night maybe a month ago I was making myself a peanut butter and jelly sandwich (I loved them as a kid and I'll love 'em till I die), when my stepson, James Carter, came into the kitchen. He asked me what I was doing; I told him; and he—as boys his age seem to invariably do—decided he was hungry too.

So I pulled everything back out, and as I started eating my sandwich, James started making his.

"Done!" he proclaimed, waving his knife with a flourish. And I had to admit it; his sandwich looked better than mine. I never seem to put on enough jelly, while his had so much the top piece of bread was threatening to slide right off.

After our peanutiest creations, we lay down on the sofa to watch TV, all snuggled up and cozy in our blanket. I'd been looking for an idea to add something to our annual tradition of passing out Walgreens gift cards to people living on the street or in need—and the blanket we were under suddenly inspired me to add blankets for that year. And what a perfect year to do that very thing, because Walgreens and CVS were both selling fleece blankets for $3.50 to $5.00 each.

So the next day I bought a bunch, and that night the family and I set out to give away a new blanket and a gift card to anyone who seemed in need of them.

After we returned home, James said to me, "You know what? This is the very best Christmas I've ever had."

The very best Christmas he'd ever had.

And why? For one reason: He gave.

So we will do this again next year. Gift cards, blankets, and . . . I know! The best peanut butter and jelly sandwiches ever made!

We say or hear "It's better to give than to receive" all the time. But how often do we actually give rather than receive? How often do we really experience just how true that saying is?

Well, if you're trying to live a regret-free life by bonding again with someone you've broken with, it's time you got back in touch with the truth about the real relationship between giving and receiving. Giving and giving all the love you have to another person isn't the only way you can ever heal with them. *It's also the only way God can keep giving and giving all of his love to you.*

Loving as God Loves

Because God is love, it's a pretty safe bet that whatever way God loves people is the way that we should try to love them also.

It's not usually thought of in this way, but I think the story of how Jesus fed the five thousand is a truly inspiring example of how he typically loved.

> As soon as Jesus heard the news [of his cousin's death], he left in a boat to a remote area to be alone. But the crowds heard where he was headed and followed on foot from many towns. Jesus saw the huge crowd as he stepped from the boat, and he had compassion on them and healed their sick.
>
> That evening the disciples came to him and said, "This is a remote place, and it's already getting late. Send the crowds away so they can go to the villages and buy food for themselves."
>
> But Jesus said, "That isn't necessary—you feed them."
>
> "But we have only five loaves of bread and two fish!" they answered.
>
> "Bring them here," he said. Then he told the people to sit down on the grass. Jesus took the five loaves and two fish, looked up toward heaven, and blessed them. Then, breaking the loaves into pieces, he gave the bread to the disciples, who distributed it to the people. They all ate as much as they wanted, and afterward, the disciples picked up twelve baskets of leftovers. About 5,000 men were fed that day, in addition to all the women and children! (Matthew 14:13–21)

The ways in which Jesus shows his love are on display in this famous story. He loved his Father in heaven, so he wanted to be alone with him. He loved the sick, so he healed them. He loved his disciples, so he challenged them to understand the role they personally could play in spreading and exemplifying love to others.

But mostly, he loved "the people." And he showed his love for them first by refusing to heed the disciples' advice to send them away, and then by (notably through his disciples) miraculously feeding them all.

And what reward did Jesus get from his generous bounty so lovingly given? What reward might he have expected in return for the loving benevolence he showed?

None. Nothing. Nada.

Zip.

Jesus' only desire was to give. He wanted nothing back in return. It was enough for him to see the people fed. That they were taken care of was all he needed to be satisfied.

It's so easy, when embroiled in any kind of struggle with another, to only think of what that struggle is costing you. *How did they hurt me?* you think. *How did they wrong me? When I showed them a measure of goodwill, when I gave them the benefit of the doubt, did they in any way show they were grateful to me for being so kind?*

"What am I getting out of this?" That's the gist of what we often think when we're in or trying to resolve a fight.

Well, next time you find yourself thinking like that, remember how Jesus fed the people. In my mind, it's almost as much a miracle that Jesus so selflessly fed them as that he fed them in the first place. If I ever miraculously fed thousands of people from nothing but five loaves of bread and a couple of fish, I would expect there to be a huge statue commemorating it on the spot the very next day, if not sooner. I would be tempted to make it all about me and not about simply feeding the people.

You may not have the ability to do the physical miracles Christ performed. But you do have what it takes to do the greatest single miracle Jesus performed over and over again: *loving selflessly.*

If you want to live a regret-free life, love others selflessly. It's that simple. And it's that miraculous.

Remembering It's Not About You

Thinking about my most recent Christmas, and what it taught my stepson about the power of selfless giving, makes me think of a much earlier Christmas in my life and what it taught me about how sometimes, no matter how much you might think something is about you, it isn't. And about how hard it can be to learn that while you've been so sure a bright spotlight is shining on you, you have, in fact, been in darkness.

I was nine. Sometime during the previous year, I had become convinced that there was no Santa Claus. I don't recall how I had come to be so sure, but I was sure. And now here it was, another week before another Christmas, and there being no Santa could only mean one thing. Somewhere, right under the very roof where I lived and upon which nary a reindeer-pulled sleigh would ever alight, were my Christmas presents.

My presents! Right in our very house! Where else could they be?

Clearly, all that remained for me was to find them.

I knew how to do few enough things when I was a kid, but the one thing I surely did know how to do was search for stuff in my house. I'd hidden in every corner; I'd climbed every counter; I'd dug around every edge of every closet and drawer. If those presents were anywhere to be found within the confines of that house, I'd find them just as sure as a moth finds a light.

The problem, of course, was arranging when to begin my hunt. There was always someone around! In order for Operation Present Find to proceed unimpeded, I definitely needed some quality time alone.

And then suddenly, about four days before Christmas, I got it. My father went one place; my mom went another; my brother went off to play with some of his friends—and presto, it was just me, all by myself in that great big, easily searchable house.

It took me about one minute to find every single present I'd be getting that year. Grouped all together, they were "hidden" under some clothes in my parents' closet that apparently (ha!) my parents thought I never went into.

There were more presents than I'd ever seen outside of a toy store, each gleaming in its box or package.

All unwrapped.

All waiting to be wrapped—and then unwrapped again by me.

It was almost too exciting. I almost couldn't look directly at my presents for fear the glowing power of them would blind me. Yet I got over that and gazed at them the way a starving man looks at a McDonald's. Heart pounding from the sheer, almost unimaginable joy of knowing all that stuff would soon be mine, I stared and stared and stared so hard I'm surprised half the presents didn't melt.

Then, sure that someone would be home before long, I reluctantly closed the closet door, went back into my room, sat on my bed, and decided to stay right there and count every moment until Christmas morning, when I'd finally be able to claim all my recently ogled booty.

Slowly but surely, as I sat there, my excitement turned to sadness.

I realized that before I'd even thought about what would happen if I saw everything ahead of time, I had ruined the very day for which those presents were intended. I'd ruined Christmas! I'd ruined it for myself directly and for my parents indirectly. For me because now I'd have to come up with some kind of fake response to act out after I opened each present. And for my parents because . . . well, because I wasn't that good an actor. They'd know.

And they did know, because, before Christmas Day, I told them I'd already seen all my presents. I didn't know what else to do. I knew I wasn't the best kid in the world, but I didn't want to be so bad as to spend half the day I was supposed to be celebrating the birth of Christ lying to everyone in my family.

It was a hard lesson, but I've never forgotten it. Oftentimes, when you think something is mostly about you, it's mostly not. It's the same with wanting to mend broken relationships. That process might seem like it's about you when, in fact, just like with me back on that Christmas so long ago, it's really about God.

CHAPTER 14

Last Words

I hope this book has helped you understand that you can live regret-free and has opened up your eyes to how to do it. A life that's truly regret-free may not be the easiest thing to achieve. But with God's love—unceasing, redemptive—keeping you clean and emotionally safe as you make your way through various important relationships, it's possible for you, and for all who call upon the Lord, to accomplish exactly that.

I was moved to write this book because if there's one thing I know about, it's having regrets. If I had a nickel for everything I've ever done that I later wished I hadn't, I would . . . well, for starters, charge the government ten cents each to buy back all of its nickels. But I know that money can't even begin to make a down payment on what really counts in life. It isn't accruing awards or accolades. It's knowing that you're okay with God, that you're pleasing to him, that you're living your life in accordance with his will and desire.

Without that, you have nothing.

Without that you have even worse than nothing. You have regrets.

The regrets I have had to call upon Jesus to help me shed are too numerous to count. But the ones that hurt the most—the ones I've had to work hardest to overcome—are those that resulted from relationships that didn't work out as I'd meant them to. I've made big blunders on the job and had judgment errors with finances, but relationships have caused me the deepest pain. With God's help I have come to understand that I was blind to my contribution to the relationship problems I've had; I simply wasn't then the man I am today.

I'm not ashamed to say that when I was younger I was less sure of who I was, of what I was to do, of who it was God wanted me to be. Like so many, I too often didn't listen to his still, quiet voice inside me, choosing instead to pay attention to the much headier and seemingly more exciting voice of opportunity before me.

I've always been such an engager of the world that usually I forgot to engage with the one who's meant to be the center of my world. While busily reaching out to others, I frequently overlooked those nearest to me; when they were reaching out, I too often wasn't there.

I am slow to learn, but I am a learner. And things are very different for me now. My wife, Misty, is a wonderful, smart, loving woman for whom I thank God every day. Today, with joy and gratitude, I do what I do, ever accompanied by the painful knowledge of mistakes I've made. I have learned much; I have no plans to repeat my failures. Now my daily intention is to pour into my marriage, like fine oil into a golden bottle, everything I've ever learned and know about relationships.

And every day I see the benefits of that pouring. I see the light in Misty's eyes, the bounce in her step, the joy with which she embraces her role as wife and mother. I see what a positive influence she is on everyone around her. I see how deeply her life is working. And I know it is in part because she knows that she is in a marriage worthy of her, one that by any measure can be called happy.

Misty and I lead lives full of stress and pressure, of course, and goodness knows we make our share of mistakes and blunders. But we truly live regret-free lives, because we don't ignore the infractions we cause or suffer, or the feelings that accompany them. We embrace them, resolve them, heal them, learn from them.

In my line of work I meet so many interesting people, from every imaginable walk of life. I meet countless folks whose hearts are breaking, who feel God has given up on them, who have themselves given up on life. Everywhere I go I find people trapped by their desires for food or sex, by low self-esteem, by a life they never even realized that they, all along the way, were fashioning for themselves. As I meet and talk with those who have attended a New Life or Women of Faith event, I am constantly moved and touched by people's strength, their resilience, their unquenchable desire to once and for all heal. People want to lead a regret-free life. And I'm deeply honored and humbled by how often, through my work, I get to play a role in the launch of that new life as they finally heed the healing call of Jesus Christ.

■ ■ ■

The difference between who I am and who I was ten years ago is that now I never forget that, as compelling and emotionally gripping as it is to guide someone as they open their heart and mind to the living God, it can't be everything to me. Now, in a private little room in my heart that I opened up for that exact purpose, I keep my wife and the family we're raising. I think of Misty's joy, her delightful spirit, the beauty that defines her inside and out. And I think of our beautiful, precious children, always ready with a smile to climb upon my lap and hear a story or watch a movie. And as excited and happy as I get watching and helping people change their perception of themselves from damaged goods to cherished guests seated at the table of Christ our Lord, I never let any of them into that private room.

That room belongs to my family. That room is where, when I'm on the road, my family and I meet. That is where we dine together in the presence of the Lord.

And always, I know, the Lord is with us all, showing us our path along a magnificent, God-centered, regret-free life.

Here's to you leading your own such life.

STEPHEN ARTERBURN is founder and chairman of New Life Ministries and host of the nation's number one Christian counseling talk show, *New Life Live!*, heard on more than 180 stations nationwide. A nationally known speaker, he has been featured on *The Oprah Winfrey Show, ABC World News Tonight*, and *CNN Live* and in the *New York Times, US News & World Report, Rolling Stone*, and many other media outlets.

Steve founded the Women of Faith conferences and is a best-selling author of more than eighty books, including the multi-million selling *Every Man's Battle* series, *Midlife Manual for Men*, and *Being Christian*. He has been nominated for numerous writing awards and won three Gold Medallion awards for writing excellence.

JOHN SHORE, an experienced writer and editor, is the author of *I'm OK—You're Not: The Message We're Sending Nonbelievers and Why We Should Stop; Penguins, Pain and the Whole Shebang*; and coauthor of *Comma Sense, Midlife Manual for Men*, and *Being Christian*. He also blogs on *Crosswalk.com*. John and his wife live in San Diego.

More Life Help From Stephen Arterburn

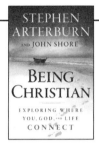

Steve Arterburn and coauthor John Shore tackle the simple, but also complex, questions that most everyone has about being a Christian. Using everyday language they offer an accessible, comprehensive, and engaging primer on the core truths of the faith in an easy-to-use format. For new and seasoned believers alike.

Being Christian by Stephen Arterburn and John Shore

Makes a great small-group study!
DVD curriculum and workbook now available!

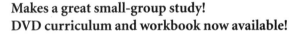

Stephen Arterburn, along with coauthor John Shore, tackle one of the most challenging—and dreaded—topics for men: midlife. Full of insight, humor, and help, *Midlife Manual for Men* prepares readers for stepping into vision, purpose, and significance in the second half of life.

Midlife Manual for Men by Stephen Arterburn and John Shore

Makes a great small-group study!
DVD curriculum and workbook now available!